Robert Lowell's Language of the Self

Robert Lowell's Language of the Self

Katharine Wallingford

The
University
of North
Carolina
Press

*Chapel Hill
and
London*

© 1988 The University of North Carolina Press
All rights reserved

Library of Congress Cataloging-in-Publication Data
Wallingford, Katharine.
  Robert Lowell's language of the self / Katharine Wallingford.
    p. cm.
  Bibliography: p.
  Includes index.
  ISBN 0-8078-1799-6 (alk. paper)
  1. Lowell, Robert, 1917–1977—Criticism and interpretation.
2. Self in literature. 3. Psychoanalysis and literature.
I. Title.
PS3523.089Z92 1988   87-37210
811'.52—dc19   CIP

The paper in this book meets the guidelines for permanence
and durability of the Committee on Production Guidelines for
Book Longevity of the Council on Library Resources.

Printed in the United States of America

92 91 90 89 88   5 4 3 2 1

Portions of Chapter 2 appeared in somewhat different form in
"Robert Lowell's Poetry of Repetition," *American Literature* 57
(1985): 424–33; portions of Chapter 1 appeared in somewhat
different form in "Robert Lowell and Free Association," *Mosaic*
19 (Fall 1986): 121–32.

Permission to reproduce quoted matter appears on pp. 169–71.

To John Martin Tapers
and Alma Entzminger Tapers

And to Monroe K. Spears

Contents

Acknowledgments

My father was a newspaperman, and the *Tallahas-see Democrat* was delivered every afternoon to my house, just alike every day and always different too. That printed object took on iconic significance in my life. Thus it is a pleasure for me, on this page of this book, to express my gratitude to my parents: my father, Jack Tapers, and my mother, Alma Tapers, who were the first to teach me about language and about love. Malcolm Johnson of the *Democrat* tried to teach me never to use a boring verb if I could avoid it. My professors at Randolph-Macon Woman's College taught me that I could do virtually anything I was willing to work hard enough at, and gave me some of the skills to do it with.

I have had a wonderfully large number of teachers and friends and editors and colleagues whose contributions to my work are many and various, and it is my pleasure to thank them here: Roy Bird, Virginia Carmichael, Susan Cashman, Susan Clark, Irvin Cohen, Terry Doody, Sandra Eisdorfer, Kristin Flanagan, Alan Grob, Iris Tillman Hill, Dennis Huston, Walter Isle, Adrienne Mayor, David Minter, Bob Patten, Janis Paul, Meredith Skura, Alan Williamson, Susan Wood, and especially Steve Axelrod and Monroe Spears.

I am grateful to Rice University for a financial contribution toward the publication of this book, as well as for sustenance of a broader nature. I am grateful also to the staffs of the Harry Ransom Humanities Research Center, University of Texas at Austin; the Houghton Library, Harvard University; and the Princeton University Library.

As Faulkner once said, "So many people are seeking something and quite often it is love." Some even find it. I would like to thank my husband, Rufus Wallingford; my daughter, Halley Wallingford; and my son, John Wallingford—they have supported me in all senses of the word, and made me laugh.

Abbreviations

D	*The Dolphin*
DBD	*Day by Day*
FLAH	*For Lizzie and Harriet*
FTUD	*For the Union Dead*
H	*History*
I	*Imitations*
LOU	*Land of Unlikeness*
LS	*Life Studies*
LWC	*Lord Weary's Castle*
MOTK	*The Mills of the Kavanaughs*
N	*Notebook*
N 1967–68	*Notebook 1967–68*
NTO	*Near the Ocean*
SP	*Selected Poems*

Robert Lowell's Language of the Self

O Sir, now do I feel myself inwrapped
On a sudden into the labyrinths
And blind beholdings of the subtle mind:
Which way to loose myself, which way to end
I know not . . .

—"John Milton's Prayer,"
an unpublished poem by Robert Lowell

Introduction:
A Poetry of
Self-Examination

ROBERT LOWELL'S friend Blair Clark, writing of the close friendship among himself, Lowell, and Frank Parker at prep school, describes their association as a "mini-phalanx that [Lowell] was head of—and there were only three members. But it had a definite moral function and he was unquestionably the leader." As a basis for their association, the three friends pledged themselves to a regimen of unmerciful self-scrutiny: "What do you do with yourself, how do you make yourself better?"[1] This commitment to self-examination, which characterized Lowell throughout his life, proved to be a driving force behind his plays and more particularly his poetry. Readers of American history and literature are not unfamiliar with this penchant for self-scrutiny: Franklin in his *Autobiography* systematically examines his faults and describes his attempts to convert them into virtues,[2] and Emerson in his journals analyzes his shortcomings and declares that it is "our duty to aim at change, at improvement, at perfection."[3] But we encounter this habit of self-examination in its purest, most extreme form in two complex systems of thought, widely separated in time and intention but united by their commitment to a program of rigorous self-examination: New England Puritanism, and its twentieth-century secular cousin, psychoanalysis. Both systems have fostered methods and ways of thinking that have become thoroughly integrated into the culture of the United States, and Robert Lowell's poetry embodies the spirit and the process of both.

Historically, both Puritanism and psychoanalysis have stressed not only the habit of self-examination, but also a concern with the process of that self-examination, and an acute awareness of the significance of language in the process. In *The New England Mind: The Seventeenth Century*, Perry Miller explains how the "doctrine of regeneration caused the founders of New England to become experts in psychological dissection." The Puritans were required constantly "to cast up their accounts" as they searched their souls for evidence of the workings of God's grace. Puritan leaders such as Thomas Hooker struggled to convey to their people the proper methods for self-examination: like the customs officer who unlocks every chest and "romages every corner," the subject must consider "all the secret conveyances, cunning contrivements, all bordering circumstances that attend the thing, the consequences of it, the nature of the causes that work it, the several occasions and provocations that lead to it, together with the end and issue that in reason is like to come of it."[4]

The Puritans' problem was that their self-examination, intended to focus attention upon and indeed to foster the submission of the self to God, often discovered instead stubborn assertions of individuality. Sacvan Bercovitch has pointed out how what seem to be simply tics of language in some of the Puritan writings—for example, "the interminable-because-unresolved incantations of the 'I' over itself"—in fact reflect dramatically the "profound Puritan ambivalence towards selfhood," an ambivalence that resulted in their "pervasive use of the personal mode."[5] Not only did the Puritans struggle incessantly and privately to determine their ultimate fate (saved or damned? saved or damned?), but the language in which they couched their accounts of the struggle of self against self had a more public dimension as well. As Edmund S. Morgan and others have taught us, the New England Puritans were the first to restrict church membership to "visible saints, to persons, that is, who had felt the stirrings of grace in their souls, and who could demonstrate this fact to the satisfaction of other saints."[6] In other words, admission to the early church depended upon one's ability to tell a convincing narrative of conversion, based at least in part upon what one had learned through self-examination.

Herbert Leibowitz, discussing Lowell's early poetry, says that "Lowell's ambivalent attitude to the Puritans is central to an understanding of his poetry. Although he repudiates them intellectually, he is at home with their buffetings and morbidity. From them he takes or rather corroborates the habit of self-examination."[7] Lowell was no undiscriminating admirer of the Puritans; on the contrary, he castigated them in *Lord Weary's Castle* for their cruelty and greed. But he was interested in their habit of searching the events of history for clues to the meaning of their own lives. Miller tells us that the Puritans "universalized their own neurasthenia,"[8] and throughout Lowell's career he would use history in a similar manner, juxtaposing self and history in ways that illuminated both. And perhaps because of his own habits of mind, he was fascinated by the Puritan penchant for obsessive introspection.

Particularly in his young manhood, Lowell was drawn to the puzzling figure of Jonathan Edwards. During the months that he spent with Allen Tate before going to Kenyon College, Lowell "was going to do a biography of Jonathan Edwards"; he "was heaping up books" on his subject, "and taking notes, and getting more and more numb on the subject," until finally he "stuck."[9] Lowell was to write three substantial poems about Edwards, "Mr. Edwards and the Spider" (*LWC* 64), "After the Surprising Conversions" (*LWC* 66), and "Jonathan Edwards in Western Massachusetts" (*FTUD* 40); in these poems he borrowed liberally from Edwards's own writings—a process of incorporation of the words of another that would continue throughout his career. And Lowell's interest in Edwards expressed itself in another significant way as well. Writing to George Santayana in January of 1948, Lowell defined himself in these terms: "I am 30, the son of a retired naval officer; J. R. Lowell was my great grand-uncle, Amy was about a fourth cousin; long long ago Jonathan Edwards was one of my ancestors."[10]

Lowell wrote this letter a little over a year before the first acute crisis of the manic-depressive illness that would plague him throughout his life—an illness that, in its manic stage, often caused the poet to assume the identity of one historical figure or another. His desire to claim Jonathan Edwards as an ancestor, when it is not clear that any such relationship existed in fact, indicates the affinity that Lowell believed existed between them, and the attraction would continue for many years. "I love you faded, / old, exiled and afraid," he would say later in "Jonathan Edwards in Western Massachusetts":

> afraid to leave
> all your writing, writing, writing
> denying the Freedom of the Will.
> You were afraid to be president
>
> of Princeton, and wrote:
> "My deffects are well known;
> I have a constitution
> peculiarly unhappy:
>
> flaccid solids,
> vapid, sizzy, scarse fluids,
> causing a childish weakness,
> a low tide of spirits.["]

Lowell's poem reflects his empathy for this "ancestor" with his obsessive writing and his "low tide of spirits," but in the earlier "Mr. Edwards and the Spider," Lowell presents a fiercer and more intimidating Edwards, fulminating at his kinsman Josiah Hawley, who is doomed to suicide and to hell.[11] In retrospect, we see that Lowell too was condemned to the hell of his manic-depressive illness and that he, like the Puritans, faced his fate with courage and did not flinch from confronting the central questions of life: "Your lacerations tell the losing game / You play against a sickness past your cure. / How will the hands be strong? How will the heart endure?"

Like Puritanism, psychoanalysis provides a process for seeking answers to these questions. The Puritans, of course, found their answers in God, but they conducted the search for these answers within their own souls. Miller quotes the Puritan leader Samuel Willard who declared, "Of all knowledge, that which concerns our selves is the most profitable." This succinct statement illustrates the close connection between Puritanism and psychoanalysis, and indeed among these two systems and the myriad forms of self-examination that have become ingrained in our culture.[12] Robert Waelder refers to "the categorical imperative of ceaseless self-exploration which provides [the] moral mainspring [of psychoanalysis],"[13] and Freud himself imagined saying to the ego, "Turn your eyes inward, look into your own depths, learn first to know yourself."[14] Stanley Leavy, discussing why and how psychoanalysis works, questions Freud's libido theory that posits a release of energy in the lifting of repression; Leavy argues instead that "the curative factor of the psychoanalytic dialogue is to be found in greater and deeper self-knowledge, realizing more and more who this is living this life in this world."[15] As we have seen from Blair Clark's description of the prep school "mini-phalanx," Lowell was predisposed to this sort of rigorous self-scrutiny, and we can well understand why he was interested when he encountered similar habits of mind in the writings of Jonathan Edwards and of Sigmund Freud.

Lowell knew Freud's work as early as 1953; he "had been reading—rather 'gulping'—Freud: 'I am a slavish convert,' he wrote to [Elizabeth] Hardwick."[16] To Allen Tate he bragged in December 1953 that he had "been reading . . . all Freud."[17] Years later he gave a perhaps more realistic account in a letter to Alan Williamson: "When I was at Iowa—'50 or later in '52—I read ⅔ of Freud, like reading Tolstoy. In that sense (memory, randomly renewed), Life Studies is full of him; a replacement to the Christian church, more intimate but without boundaries or credo, or philosophy. . . . I picked up Freud from reading, talk (I knew about his way of thinking vividly from Delmore Schwartz before I read a word)."[18] As he indicated in an interview in 1965, Lowell took seriously Freud's influence on the culture in general and on himself in particular:

> Well, I get a funny thing from psycho-analysis. I mean Freud is the man who moves me most: and his case histories, and the book on dreams, read almost like a late Russian novel to me—with a scientific rather than a novelist's mind. They have a sort of marvellous old-order quality to them, though he is the father of the new order, almost the opposite of what psycho-analysis has been since. . . . There is something rather beautiful and sad and intricate about Freud that seems to have gone out of psycho-analysis; it's become a way of looking at things. . . . Freud seems the only religious teacher. I have by no means a technical understanding of Freud, but he's very much part of my life. He seems unique among the

non-fictional teachers of the century. He's a prophet. I think
somehow he continues both the Jewish and Christian tradi-
tion, and puts it maybe in a much more rational position. I
find nothing bores me more than someone who has all the
orthodox sort of Freudian answers like the Catechism, but
what I find about Freud is that he provides the conditions that
one must think in. . . . The two thinkers, non-fictional think-
ers, who influence and are never out of one's mind are Marx
and Freud.[19]

As this interview suggests, although Lowell admired and re-
spected Freud's works, he was ambivalent about the value of psy-
choanalysis. And this ambivalence imbues the few poems he
wrote in which he specifically talks about Freud. In *Life Studies*, in
"To Delmore Schwartz (Cambridge 1946)," Lowell makes gentle
fun of the two young, intense poets, "Underseas fellows, nobly
mad," who "talked away our friends. 'Let Joyce and Freud, / the
Masters of Joy, / be our guests here,' you said" (53). Although he
relished the bilingual pun on "Freud" and "Joy," he knew well the
irony of the pun and used the character of Freud in a more somber
way in "Death and the Bridge" (*N* 141). This poem is a meditation
on a macabre "landscape" by Frank Parker that serves as the fron-
tispiece for *Notebook*. In the picture, against the background of
"the eternal, provincial / city Dante saw as Florence and hell," a
skeleton is borne on the back of a horse across a "bridge of red
railtie girders." "We will follow our skeletons on the girder, / out
of life and Boston," the poet predicts, "singing with Freud: /
'God's ways are dark and very seldom pleasant.' " "God's ways are
dark" indeed in Lowell's last two poetic treatments of Freud. In
"Freud" (*D* 46), the old doctor himself, exiled and lonely in Lon-
don, is on his own way "out of life." In "Three Freuds" (*DBD* 112),
the poet, entering a mental hospital as a patient, notices the
"bearded marble bust" of the hospital's founder and the "live pa-
tient" plucking up "coleslaw in his hands." Both look to the poet
like Freud, and none of the three can help him; when he emerges
from the hospital, "it may seem too late."

Although Lowell absorbed Freud's ideas from his own reading
and more generally from the culture of the time, it was through
the poet's manic-depressive illness that he felt most acutely the
influence of Freud, and that influence was more one of method or

process than of theory. Lowell was in psychotherapy time and again throughout his life, but apparently he was never psychoanalyzed in an orthodox Freudian manner; in his letter to Williamson, he said that he had never "been psychoanalysed" or "suffered an emotional or intellectual transference in therapy."[20] But the influence of psychoanalysis is pervasive and its techniques have been widely adapted by psychiatrists practicing other types of therapy. At any rate, as we have seen, the poet was predisposed to self-examination, and the specific therapies must only have reinforced his own habits of mind. It is impossible and unnecessary to know to what extent Lowell integrated his readings of Freud and his own experiences with psychotherapy, but thanks in large part to Ian Hamilton's biography, we are able to trace in rough outline the progression of Lowell's attitudes toward and experiences with psychiatrists.

If we can accept as accurate the portrayal of Lowell in Jean Stafford's autobiographical short story "An Influx of Poets," the young Lowell during the time of his marriage to Stafford expressed a "diehard repudiation of psychiatry as poppycock, a Viennese chicanery devised to bilk idle women and hypochondriacal men."[21] Lowell knew at least one psychiatrist early in his life: "Dr. Merrill Moore, the family psychiatrist" ("Unwanted," DBD 121), whom Lowell's mother consulted about her son as early as 1935, when Lowell was in prep school at St. Mark's.[22] Mrs. Lowell's relationship with Moore was to be long and complicated, and it is not clear whether Moore ever thought of Robert Lowell as his patient rather than as the troubled son of Charlotte Lowell. In any event, shortly thereafter he helped to change the course of Lowell's life. By that time Lowell was a student at Harvard, where he had written some poems and fallen in love. After a series of arguments with his parents about his desire to marry, Lowell hit his father and knocked him to the ground—an event that was later to figure largely in his poetry. Moore acted as mediator between Lowell and his parents, and in fact was responsible for Lowell's meeting Ford Madox Ford, who in turn arranged for Lowell to visit Allen Tate in Tennessee. Thus in the spring of 1937 Lowell headed south to Tate and John Crowe Ransom, and thence to Kenyon College, the classics, Randall Jarrell and Peter Taylor, and the real beginning of his poetic career.

Although Moore continued to be involved in Lowell's life in the years thereafter, primarily through his relationship with Charlotte Lowell, it appears that his motives were not unmixed with regard to the young poet. He served as Lowell's guardian for a brief period in 1939; Hamilton suggests that "Moore's main interest . . . seems to have been to impress Charlotte Lowell with his astute handling of a tricky situation." And in 1953 Moore wrote "an odd letter to Elizabeth Hardwick, suggesting that he and Charlotte might collaborate in writing 'a book about Bobby, titled background of a poet, dealing with his early life up to the day he left Boston to go south.'" Besides raising troublesome questions about exploitation and professional ethics, the proposal establishes Moore without question as a member of the Charlotte Lowell camp in the ongoing adversary relation between son and mother: "Bobby" was the son the family wanted, while Lowell by this time was calling himself "Cal."

Aside from the fact that it was Moore who directed Lowell to the South and to Tate in 1937, his influence on the poet is problematic. Certainly the reader who looks at any of Moore's several books of sonnets thinks immediately of Lowell's years-long obsession with the sonnet form and wonders if there is any connection between the two. In a statement at the beginning of M, Moore says that "these thousand sonnets are part of a larger work begun some years ago, still in progress, and which may never be completed. At present the unfinished work comprises some 50,000 sonnets."[23] It is tempting to speculate on the habits of mind that impelled both Moore and Lowell to write the kind of poetry they did; indeed, we shall indulge in that speculation with respect to Lowell throughout this book. For the present, however, let us confine ourselves to noticing what we shall call a coincidence. Keeping in mind Lowell's Notebook, consider Moore's description of his own book in the statement at its beginning:

> The very nature of the work is paradoxical; although the individual units are compressed, the scheme itself is expansive. Since it reflects the casual and contradictory elements of life, it is impromptu, informal, even haphazard. It is not a fusion but a diffusion; not fixed, but untameable, unpredictable, explosive.
>
> The sonnets themselves fall into two natural divisions: those presenting the outer experiences, autobiography of the

flesh, and those reflecting the inner events, the autobiography of the spirit.

The autobiographical sonnets of *Notebook* cannot be separated into categories: for Lowell, inner and outer experiences often merge; but in all other respects, Moore's description of his own book describes Lowell's as well.

Lowell himself was ambivalent about Moore and in his last volume of poems took a more charitable view of the doctor than one might expect. In "Unwanted" (*DBD* 121), he describes him in these terms:

> Dr. Merrill Moore, the family psychiatrist,
> had unpresentable red smudge eyebrows,
> and no infirmity for tact—
> in his conversation or letters,
> each phrase a new
> paragraph,
> implausible as the million
> sonnets he rhymed into his dictaphone,
> or dashed on windshield writing-pads,
> while waiting out a stoplight—
> scattered pearls, some true.
> Dead he is still a mystery,
> once a crutch to writers in crisis.
> I am two-tongued, I will not admit
> his Tennessee rattling saved my life.

Up to this point the doctor is presented as an amiable eccentric, and Lowell's "scattered pearls, some true" seems an accurate judgment on Moore's poetry; but the next lines raise disturbing questions:

> Did he become mother's lover
> and prey
> by rescuing her from me?
> He was thirteen years her junior . . .
> When I was in college, he said, "You know
> you were an unwanted child?"
> Was he striking my parents to help me?   [Lowell's ellipsis]

Lowell gives us no answers to the questions raised in "Unwanted," and, indeed, the question of Moore's influence on Lowell diminishes almost to insignificance when considered against the tumultous background of the cycles of mania and depression that racked Lowell's life. In the beginning, after the first hospitalizations, Lowell lost his scorn for psychiatry and hoped forlornly that psychotherapy would cure him. Writing to George Santayana in December 1949, Lowell described his experience at the Payne-Whitney Clinic of New York Hospital in these terms:

> The *mystical* experiences and explosions turned out to be pathological. . . . In September it got so bad that I had to go to a hospital and take psycho-therapy. There I have been ever since, but am about done and am living half in and half out of the hospital.
>
> During all that blind mole's time—the fascinated spirit watching the holocaust of irrationality—apathy tormenting apathy—somehow I couldn't write you.[24]

For the reader who knows the history of Lowell's life, it wrings the heart to read the poet's perception, in 1949, that he is "about done" with the hospitals and the therapy.

Writing in a wholly different mood to his cousin Harriet Winslow in 1956, Lowell tells an anecdote about William Carlos Williams that reveals a cheerful tolerance of psychoanalysis—at least as applied to another rather than to himself:

> I'm sad this morning because I have just seen William Carlos Williams off. . . . Since I last saw him, he has nearly died four times, been psycho-analysed (at the age of sixty-nine and on Merrill Moore's advice) been partially paralysed, and he might die suddenly any day. All this gnaws at him, and since he is a doctor, there is nothing that he can hide from himself. Still he is very gloriously alive, and says he had always had a Mother-complex (his mother died three years ago) and no sense at all before his analysis.[25]

Then in 1958 he wrote the saddest letter of all, another letter to his "dearest Cousin Harriet": "The future is much less alarming than might have been feared. I have a very good doctor whom I'll be seeing regularly. We both feel and think that these attacks can be permanently cured by therapy. Elizabeth and I have good times ahead, and little Harriet will never see the shadow that has darkened us and gone. I don't think this is whistling in the dark; we have a great store of sympathy and much has been learned."[26] But the shadow was to return again and again; Lowell was to see hospitals and doctors for the rest of his life.

After Lowell began taking lithium in 1967, he placed all his hope in that newly discovered drug. Writing to Alan Williamson in 1974, the poet announced that "I have never taken [Freud] as gospel, been psychoanalysed, suffered an emotional or intellectual transference in therapy—my own decisive trouble was, as with all manics, a *salt* deficiency."[27] And Robert Giroux says that of all his conversations with Lowell he remembers "most vividly Cal's words about the new drug, lithium carbonate, which had such good results and gave him reason to believe he was cured: 'It's terrible, Bob, to think that all I've suffered, and all the suffering I've caused, might have arisen from the lack of a little salt in my brain.' "[28] This attitude was of course a drastic oversimplification, but in a 1982 review of Sylvia Plath's *Collected Poems*, Helen Vendler echoes Lowell's late rejection of psychotherapy: "We are more conscious now of the physiological causes of (and remedies for) depression, thanks to poets like Lowell, who have expressed considerable irony about the sedulous efforts of therapists to ascribe to environmental causes what turns out to be a lack of lithium."[29] But just as Lowell was inevitably disillusioned by psychotherapy's failure to effect a permanent cure, so was he forced to learn that lithium would prove no panacea either; although it acted initially to moderate the course of Lowell's illness, he was never to be "cured," never to be free from the threat of mania and its aftermath, crippling depression.

How, then, did Robert Lowell bear the life he was given to live? In *Freud and Man's Soul*, Bruno Bettelheim argues that the English translators of Freud misrepresent his work when they translate the German *die Seele* as "mind" rather than "soul." Although *die Seele* had for Freud no religious connotations, says Bettelheim, the founder of psychoanalysis intended by the term "man's essence . . . that which is most spiritual and worthy in man," and psychoanalysis teaches us how we may discover that essence: "this demanding and potentially dangerous voyage of self-discovery will result in our becoming more fully human, so that we may no longer be enslaved without knowing it to the dark forces that reside in us."[30] Gabriel Pearson believes that Lowell's poetic career "imitates" such a voyage: "Lowell's poetic career imitates—in an Aristotelian sense—the progress of self-therapy and thereby proposes itself as a case of an ultimately viable existence. It becomes exemplary as a measure of the depth and intensity of the forces that batter the self from within and without, and describes the forms that resistance to these can assume."[31] The form that Lowell's resistance to the dark forces assumed was poetic form, was language trans-formed. He loved words—he posited as our common ancestor "Orpheus in Genesis," who "hacked words from brute sound, and taught men English" ("In Genesis," *H* 26)—and he was a prodigal user of language. He talked a lot, he taught his students, he wrote loving letters to his family and friends, he wrote plays, and always, incessantly, he wrote poetry. He wrote, rewrote, revised, revised again, poem after poem. And in a more self-conscious way than any of our other great poets, he sought to discover himself in his poetry.

After his mother's death in 1954, Lowell's doctors suggested as a therapeutic measure that he write down what he could remember of his childhood; so Lowell began writing a series of prose reminiscences that would eventually become the basis for *Life Studies*.[32] Lowell had specific results in mind when he undertook the project: "I am writing my autobiography literally to 'pass the time.' I almost doubt if the time would pass at all otherwise. However, I also hope the result will supply me with swaddling clothes, with a sort of immense bandage of grace and ambergris for my hurt nerves."[33] Of course Lowell is not the first poet to seek relief from "hurt nerves" through his art, and we need not examine theories of sublimation or catharsis in order to agree with Philip Rieff that, "having shaped and ordered aesthetically his psychic burden, the artist has already acted therapeutically upon himself."[34] If these theories of art as therapy (among many other things, of course) are relevant to all writers, they are summed up and embodied in Robert Lowell and his poetry. Because of a unique coincidence of temperament and circumstance, he spent his life writing poems that explore the question "Is getting well ever an art, / or art a way to get well?" ("Unwanted," *DBD* 121).

"Lowell's habits of mind are intrinsically psychological," Alan

Williamson tells us; "he is intensely self-observant, and always inclined to connect conscious thought processes with the dream-like, the infantile, the anatomical."[35] Speaking of *Life Studies*, Williamson says that "if any one structure of thought has replaced Catholicism as Lowell's source of methods and values, it is psychoanalysis; his goal is self-understanding, and his principal techniques—the resurrection of early memories, the unsparing objectivity about present behavior, and the increased conscious awareness of interpersonal dynamics—are all common features of the analytic experience."[36]

Although Williamson goes on to say parenthetically that "there is a more direct dependence on specific Freudian insights in many individual poems," his emphasis is on the analytic *experience*—the methods and techniques of analysis rather than what one may learn as a result of the process. Meredith Skura makes the same distinction in *The Literary Use of the Psychoanalytic Process*:

> My emphasis on process draws attention to psychoanalysis as a method rather than as a body of knowledge, as a way of interpreting rather than as a specific product or interpretation. I am interested in psychoanalysis not so much for what it reveals about human nature, or even about the particular human being presently on the couch, but for the way in which it reveals anything at all. A sensitivity to the delicate changes in consciousness taking place moment by moment in the actual process of an analytic hour can lead to a renewed awareness of the possibilities of language and narrative—an awareness that will increase our range of discriminations rather than reduce them to a fixed pattern, as the theory tends to do. The dynamic movement of the process brings us closer to what goes on in literature than the theory, with its rigid hypostatizations, can ever come.[37]

In suggesting that we may learn something about how literature works by looking at how psychoanalysis works, Skura is directing her remarks to people who read stories and poems, yet the same reasoning applies to those who write the stories and poems as well.

Psychoanalysis, or self-examination of any sort, implies a splitting of the self into that part which is to examine and that part which is to be examined; in Otto Fenichel's succinct description, the ego is split into "an observing and an experiencing part so that the former can judge the irrational character of the latter."[38] Fenichel's "experiencing part," in an analysis, is "irrational" because it has been set free from the control of the rational and allowed—indeed, encouraged—to roam freely. Skura describes the process as one in which "one part of the mind is freely associating" while the other part, the "observer," often "draws on the resources of logic and secondary process thinking discarded by free association, but its role is not to provide authoritative interpretation. . . . Instead, it provides new perspectives, finds new relationships, reorganizes figure and ground, and changes emphasis." She associates this characteristic of the psychoanalytic process with literature: the "resemblance between psychoanalysis and literature lies in their dynamic interaction: the interaction between the free-ranging play of mind and the organizing response to it, and the continuing play which they contradict or confirm."[39] Again, Skura is talking about critical activity, the reading of literature; and, again, we may extend her remarks to apply to the writing of literature as well. In her novel *Mrs. Stevens Hears the Mermaids Singing*, May Sarton has the young poet Hilary Stevens explain to her governess that "a writer not only feels but watches himself feeling."[40] Ernst Kris applies this same concept to artists: "The process [of artistic creation] involves a continual interplay between creation and criticism, manifested in the painter's alternation of working on the canvas and stepping back to observe the effect. We may speak here of a *shift in psychic level*, consisting in the fluctuation of functional regression and control."[41]

Although Kris is speaking of artistic creation in a spatial medium—painting—many critics have found in Lowell's poetry signs of a similar duality, which Jay Martin describes as "the analytic faculty of the poet's imagination overhearing the secrets of his personality."[42] Several critics discuss this quality of double perspective in terms of a dichotomy between "inside" and "outside." In Marjorie Perloff's words, Lowell is "able to stand outside his own history and to evaluate it with some ironic detachment."[43] We can agree with Robert Hass that Lowell is "outside the picture" in "Waking Early Sunday Morning" (*NTO* 13) but "in it" in "The Quaker Graveyard in Nantucket" (*LWC* 14).[44] Gabriel Pearson, discussing Lowell's use of the old South Boston Aquarium in "For the

Union Dead" (*FTUD* 70), notes that "Lowell sees himself simultaneously on both sides of the glass at once, within and without, feeling over its surfaces and seeing himself as so feeling from the other side."[45] Steven Gould Axelrod, describing "Lowell's inner-outer view of his past self" in *Life Studies*, refers to "his use of a narratorial double-consciousness; the authorial awareness includes both the consciousness of the remembered child [inside the picture] and that of the remembering adult poet [outside the picture]."[46]

Lowell's "double vision" is not confined to the early work. John Simon, chastising Lowell for his *Imitations*, complains that he has botched the translation of Rilke's "Orpheus, Eurydice and Hermes" (100). In the original poem, Rilke has Orpheus's senses "cleft in two," his sight running ahead of him, and his hearing "trailing backward toward her whom he must not look at."[47] Perhaps because he is aware of his own divided ego, Lowell changes the sense of the lines: "It was as though his intelligence were cut in two. / His outlook worried like a dog behind him, / now diving ahead, now romping back, / now yawning on its haunches at an elbow of the road." The Rilke imitation shows us that the observing ego can be playful as well as serious, can participate actively rather than merely attend. But its more common guise is that of the serious, rational observer, as in this description by John Crick of the two elements in *Notebook*: "the shaping surface, with its uncompromising pattern of fourteen lines, its rational, objective observer, and its world of ideas and things; and the subconscious drama welling up, the experiencing sub-world."[48] And Alan Williamson gives us yet another sort of observing ego when he points out, in the late poems, the "curious, joyful feeling of being—not in the ordinary sense—beside himself, beside his own life."[49]

Does this split in the ego of the poet, as we encounter it in Lowell's poetry, serve an aesthetic or a more personal purpose? Does it shape and form raw material into art, or does it act to further the poet's self-knowledge? To pose the questions in this either-or form is to understand the futility of trying to answer them: it is impossible to separate the strands of self-examination from the strands of art in Lowell's poetry, and, indeed, their interdependence fortified both his life and his writing. The splitting of the ego into two parts, then, has itself a dual function: it permits the rational "observing ego" to observe the experiencing self, and to shape the materials of the experience into art. Each function enters into and affects the other. Meredith Skura, in a passage quoted earlier, describes how the observing ego "provides new perspectives, finds new relationships, reorganizes figure and ground, and changes emphasis"; in Lowell's poem "Beyond the Alps" (*LS* 3), we can ourselves observe the observing ego as it performs these tasks.

"Beyond the Alps" begins *Life Studies*, and the name of the volume is instructive. The study of a life is a process; as the poem makes clear, it is the life of Robert Lowell—the experiencing self—that is being studied, and the observer self of Robert Lowell does the studying. The poem begins, as Irvin Ehrenpreis remarks, "with what look like random associations suggesting the real flow of a unique consciousness."[50] The poet is both on a train, reading a newspaper while making a journey, and outside the train, watching:

> Reading how even the Swiss had thrown the sponge
> in once again and Everest was still
> unscaled, I watched our Paris pullman lunge
> mooning across the fallow Alpine snow.

Wyatt Prunty suggests that the train's "motion is analogous to Lowell's consciousness making constant revisions between a known past and an expected and unfolding future."[51] His comment reminds us that many psychoanalysts stress the importance of the subject's ability to make out of the materials dredged up from the unconscious a personal narrative, a history that feels true. In this poem, the poet is making a journey through time and space from the Rome of his early Roman Catholicism to Paris, "our black classic," where he will have need of the new perspectives and new relationships that the observing ego can discern. "Life changed to landscape," he tells us. "Much against my will / I left the City of God where it belongs." Behind him he has left, among other things, the pope, who has just "defined the dogma of Mary's bodily assumption" into heaven. The "old," believing Lowell might have accepted this dogma, but the "new," ironic Lowell has a different perspective:

The lights of science couldn't hold a candle
to Mary risen—at one miraculous stroke,
angel-wing'd, gorgeous as a jungle bird!
But who believed this? Who could understand?

Reorganizing figure and ground in a literal way, the observing Lowell tells us that "our mountain-climbing train had come to earth"; changing emphasis, no longer aspiring to unreachable heights, he says in a wry voice: "There were no tickets for that altitude / once held by Hellas." The poet who, in the early lines of the poem, had watched the train lunge forward, now turns around and watches, from a different perspective, "each backward, wasted Alp." And meanwhile, what of the experiencing self? "Tired of the querulous hush-hush of the wheels, / the bleareyed ego kicking in my berth / lay still." The ego is observing itself, and out of this process poetry is being written.

In order to talk about the mind and its "contents," we use what Skura calls "the most basic metaphors of [Freud's] system, the ones that take the mind to be a space, ideas to be things, and emotions to be substances which can be dammed up or can overflow."[52] Lowell uses these metaphors to great effect. "From now on, my mind's autumn!" he translates from Baudelaire. "I must take / the field and dress my beds with spade and rake / and restore order to my flooded grounds" ("The Ruined Garden," I 52). The mind as ruined garden becomes, in "Waking Early Sunday Morning," the mind as cluttered woodshed: "put old clothes on, and explore / the corners of the woodshed for / its dregs and dreck" (NTO 13). In a letter to Harriet Winslow, the mind becomes "my study" (a wonderful pun), and Lowell uses other metaphors for the activity of the mind in exploring itself: "I have been thinking a lot about people and moments in the past. A lot is lost, and a lot was never seen or understood. . . . Still it's fascinating to see what one can fish up, clear up, and write down—it's like cleaning my study, like going perhaps to some chiropractor, who leaves me with all my original bones jumbled back in a new and sounder structure."[53]

The chiropractor, if he is not a psychiatrist, must surely be a relative of the observing, organizing part of the ego, who "provides new perspectives, finds new relationships, reorganizes figure and ground, and changes emphasis." Lowell has been "thinking," he says; it is fascinating to see what one can "fish up, clear up, write down." Besides indicating that for Lowell self-examination and writing are parts of the same process, his statement suggests another useful metaphor. When Lowell speaks of seeing what he can "fish up," or when Freudians refer to the emotions as substances that can be dammed up or can overflow, they are using the common metaphor of the unconscious as a body of water.

"Children, the raging memory drools / Over the glory of past pools," Lowell says in "The Drunken Fisherman" (*LWC* 37), and throughout his career he identified with both the fisherman on the bank and the creatures beneath the water. We have already noticed that, in "For the Union Dead" (*FTUD* 70), "Lowell sees himself simultaneously on both sides of the glass at once, within and without," and the poet admits in that poem, "I often sigh still / for the dark downward and vegetating kingdom / of the fish and reptile." Gabriel Pearson has described Lowell as "seeming always submarine, as if he was looking out at the world though the windows of a fishtank."[54] Indeed, Lowell seems always to have had ready access to some submarine world. A surrealistic prose piece that he wrote while a student at Harvard begins with the words "Sometimes, when we are in disorder, every pinprick and scraping blade of grass magnifies." From there he moves through a series of associations to a "grass tide": "The sea lay grass green and ever so serene. Sharks' fins ripped the ripe slick. . . . Whales spouted, and their flat tails flopped and towered, making me conscious of umbrageous trunks surrounding the sea; a Nether World or antideluvian scene; shimmer of shiners, floating logs and submerged shadows."[55] Although sometimes Lowell's watery worlds are inhabited by such beneficent beings as dolphins, more often the sea creatures are dark and threatening. From the bloodless corpse and mutilated whale of "The Quaker Graveyard in Nantucket" (*LWC* 14) through the murderous shark circling "visibly behind the window" at the end of "Ulysses and Circe" (*DBD* 3), Lowell dredges up the monsters who live in the unconscious.

If we apprehend the mind as a space, the unconscious as a sea, and ideas as things like monsters, how do we talk about the conscious mind, that part of the mind-space which is not the sea? Freud insisted that "in psycho-analysis we take spatial ways of looking at things seriously. For us the ego is really something superficial and the id something deeper—looked at from outside, of course. The ego lies between reality and the id."[56] Gabriel Pearson has used these related metaphors to talk about Lowell's poetry: "A Lowell poem . . . never looks other than fragile, friable, only just mastering the pulls and pressures that threaten to disintegrate it. Freud's view of the ego as a hard won layer of self that achieves enough stability to curb—and yet be fed and thickened by—the importunate, blind drives of the id and that copes and transacts with external reality seems apposite."[57] The early poems in particular *contain* so much turmoil that they seem "suffused with a violent—almost a caricatural—emotionalism, as the buried feelings assume control over reality."[58] M. L. Rosenthal, observing this kind of suffused emotionalism, has associated it with T. S. Eliot's discussion of the lack, in *Hamlet*, of an objective correlative, his reference to the "intense feeling, ecstatic or terrible, without an object or exceeding its object," which "is something which every person of sensibility has known."[59] Hans Loewald explains this disparity between feeling and object when he states that our "present, current experiences have intensity and depth to the extent to which they are in communication (interplay) with the unconscious, infantile experiences representing the indestructable matrix of all subsequent experiences."[60] And Skura explains the power of fantasy in similar terms: the fantasy, which may exist, of course, in the form of a poem, "does not replace adult experience but instead brings the intensities of childhood experience to bear on current adult life."[61]

The infantile experience of such great intensity to which Skura and Loewald refer will often have been an experience of conflict, of unfulfilled desire. Waelder declares that analysis "tries to inch backward from the conflicts of the present to the childhood experiences to which they are related." For Waelder, psychoanalysis "tries to undo the repressions and thereby to restore to consciousness the full conflict as it had probably been conscious, if only for a fleeting moment, and as it would be conscious had the individual not been unwilling or unable to face up to it, and not tried to escape from it by repression."[62] Fenichel gives the orthodox Freudian view as he describes the conflict as one between id and ego:

Thus we have . . . first a defense of the ego against an instinct, then a conflict between the instinct striving for discharge and the defensive forces of the ego, then a state of damming up, and finally the neurotic symptoms which are distorted discharges as a consequence of the state of damming up—a compromise between the opposing forces. The symptom is the only step in this development that becomes manifest; the conflict, its history, and the significance of the symptoms are unconscious.[63]

And, finally, Philip Rieff translates the conflict into the wider terms of *Civilization and Its Discontents*, in which Freud "conceives of the self . . . as the subject of a struggle between two objective forces—unregenerate instincts and overbearing culture. Between these two forces there may be compromise but no resolution. Since the individual can neither extirpate his instincts nor wholly reject the demands of society, his character expresses the way in which he organizes and appeases the conflict between the two."[64]

Lowell, like the rest of us, must have had buried conflicts whose energy and intensity was transferred to and evoked by experiences in his adult life. Here we are not concerned with what those experiences, infantile or adult, may have been, but rather with the way in which Lowell used the feelings evoked by these experiences in his poetry. Conflict of which he was conscious seemed rather to fuel his energy than to drain it. In a wonderful reminiscence written after Lowell's death, his friend Peter Taylor demonstrates how Lowell seemed to thrive on contradiction and conflict: "Once he had participated in something, he was never willing to give up his part in it—not even old opinions that no longer suited him. In a sense, he was a Roman Catholic to the end, and would say so, though he would also almost simultaneously declare that he was in no sense a believer. He would boast at times that he had never lost a friend. He never even wanted to give up a marriage entirely."[65]

"A poem needs to include a man's contradictions," Lowell said,[66] and the ability to hold two contradictory opinions at once, to be on both sides of a conflict simultaneously, is a salient feature of his poetry. Alan Williamson, discussing the many ways in which Lowell was "self-divided," insists that "one will not understand the whole man, or the whole achievement, if one excludes either side of the dialectic."[67] Richard Fein, in a remark that seems particularly apt for our study of psychoanalytic techniques in Lowell's poetry, says that *Notebook* and *History* "seem to be hoping that turmoil will reveal something significant—some keys if not *the* key—if one only persists in writing about unresolvable tendencies and mixed feelings."[68]

Lowell's use of conflict in his poetry has a public dimension as well. According to Axelrod, "The Quaker Graveyard in Nantucket" (*LWC* 14) is "a field of conflict between opposing forces within the poet's psyche, and by extension within the collective psyche of our civilization."[69] Randall Jarrell, in his fine essay on the early poetry, illuminates *Lord Weary's Castle* in these terms:

> Underneath all these poems "there is one story and one story only." . . . The poems understand the world as a sort of conflict of opposites. In this struggle one opposite is that cake of custom in which all of us lie embedded like lungfish—the stasis or inertia of the stubborn self, the obstinate persistence in evil that is damnation. Into this realm of necessity the poems push everything that is closed, turned inward, incestuous, that blinds or binds. . . . But struggling within this like leaven, falling to it like light, is everything that is free or open, that grows or is willing to change.[70]

When Jarrell sees, in *Lord Weary's Castle*, "the world as a sort of conflict of opposites," he is surely describing the struggle within the smaller world of the poet himself as well. Although Jarrell sees a movement in the poems toward a resolution on one side or the other of the conflict, within the poet himself it is not the resolution but the struggle itself, the process of examination of self and world, that gives such energy to the poetry.

Hayden Carruth said it best: "A man's being, fought for, fragment by fragment, there on the page: this we can recognize."[71] "One life, one writing," Lowell said in "Night Sweat" (*FTUD* 68), and it is hard to read the poetry because it was hard to live the life. "Looking over my *Selected Poems*, about thirty years of writing," Lowell reflected, "my impression is that the thread that strings it together is my autobiography, it is a small-scale *Prelude*, written in many different styles and with digressions, yet a continuing story—still wayfaring."[72] But when Lowell speaks of autobiography as the "thread" that "strings" his poetry together, we must be careful not to seduce ourselves into thinking that either

Lowell's person or his poetry can be reduced to a tidy, unified narrative. As twentieth-century readers, we are accustomed to think of the self as a fragile construct at best, in Jane Gallop's words, "an illusion done with mirrors."[73] Lowell's poetry reflects that tenuous fragility.[74] Both Charles Altieri and Karl Malkoff point to the famous lines "I myself am hell; / nobody's here" ("Skunk Hour," LS 89) as indications of a lack of sense of self; the self, in Malkoff's words, "has lost control, has abandoned its role of arbiter of experience to the extent that that center of consciousness seems no longer to exist."[75]

Lowell's title Life Studies is particularly interesting in this regard; we have spoken earlier of the volume as a narrative of a journey of self-examination, the study of a life, but in its strict sense the title refers to quick sketches, unfinished, discrete. Contemporary psychoanalysts and therapists disagree on the extent to which a coherent narrative of one's life is the goal of psychotherapy; Jacques Lacan speaks of the necessity of achieving "the intersubjective continuity of the discourse in which the subject's history is constituted," but Roy Schafer and others have deemphasized such a continuity.[76] As we shall see, during much of his life Lowell vacillated between earnestly trying to fashion such a narrative and strenuously resisting any such attempt. But by the time of The Dolphin and Day by Day, he seems to have decided that any story of his life would be provisional, that "the past changes more than the present" ("To Frank Parker," DBD 91), that he can settle for discontinuous glimpses rather than trying to force his memories into a coherent narrative.

Of Lowell's lack of a stable identity, Jay Martin says that "what could be held together, poetry held."[77] This poetry of Lowell's, as we have seen, was inextricably bound up with the process of self-examination; in this process he used techniques commonly used in psychoanalysis and other types of psychotherapy. In the following chapters we will consider, through close readings of the poetry, Lowell's use of specific techniques of psychoanalysis: free association, repetition or "working-through," deliberate concentration on the relation between the poet and the "other" to whom he addresses himself, and the use of memory to probe the past. Of course to divide the psychoanalytic process into components for the purpose of discussion is to falsify the way it works, because its essence is the free flow of ideas and associations in no logical order and with no clear demarcation between specific techniques. The poet working alone on a poem, the psychoanalyst and patient working together in an analysis, and the literary critic working with the texts of others all use words as the instruments of their work, and are often frustrated by the limitations of language, the sense that it acts to suppress and limit truth as often as to reveal and further it. But even Freud acknowledged that "we have no way of conveying knowledge of a complicated set of simultaneous events except by describing them successively; and thus it happens that all our accounts are at fault to begin with owing to one-sided simplification and must wait till they can be supplemented, built on to, and so set right."[78] Or as right as we can get them.

1

A Poetry of Association

IN A LETTER he wrote in 1949 to George Santayana in Rome, Robert Lowell describes a process of thought that sounds remarkably like the psychoanalytic technique of free association:

Dear Mr. Santayana:

I was just nodding and I saw an image of a fat, yellowish dog receding down the center of a country road—the center was grass and the ruts clam-shells; so much for flux.

I had hoped to send you a book of my poems as a sort of Christmas present; but no. One thing written brings up another—somewhat as the *dog-image*. Should one shut these things out? It seems safer to let them come, take one's time, to be helpless. . . .

Vocation is love, I think: for beauty, or the Muses, or what you wish. . . . Now at 31 it's just there—I can't send it away for long or find alternatives. There's the power side, the making side, the craft one learns. But now I am struck by the other, the *powerless*—powerless, when it does not come; most of all powerless, when it does, like the dog taking you God knows where![1]

When Lowell pays attention to images that pop into his mind unbidden like the yellow dog, when he determines not to "shut these things out" but to "let them come," when he asserts his willingness to follow along as the dog takes him "God knows where," he might well be describing what Jacques Lacan has called "the forced labour of this discourse without escape, on which the psychologist (not without humour) and the therapist (not without cunning) have bestowed the name of 'free association.' "[2] Free association is a "forced labour" indeed, because in order to sneak through the bars of repression and gain access to the unconscious, a subject must be willing, in Freud's words, to "entirely renounce any critical selection . . . and say whatever comes into his head," to follow his associations wherever they lead, no matter how unpleasant such a process may be.[3]

If we can judge by a prose piece written while he was a student at Harvard, Lowell seems always to have been willing to submit himself to the uncontrolled flow of associational thinking:

Sometimes, when we are in disorder, every pinprick and scraping blade of grass magnifies. A pebble rolls into the Rock of Gibraltar. I got a sunstroke regarding the gardener mow the lawn. He dumped matted green grass into a canvas bag and emptied the bag into a rut pond behind a clump of shrubbery. . . . I watched him dump grass on the surface where there ought to have been frogs. I smelled the odor of dried verdure in my sleep; tons of it, wet and lifeless, floating and stifling. At morning the grass tide rose up gruesome.[4]

This sketch develops into an impression of the ominous "Nether World or antideluvian scene; shimmer of shiners, floating logs and submerged shadows" that we discussed in connection with Lowell's attraction to things of the sea. Later, in a draft of a piece he then called "The Balanced Aquarium," Lowell described the strong pull of the submarine, what we may interpret as the unconscious breaking through into consciousness:

One morning in July of 1954 I sat brooding by the open door of my bedroom on the third floor of the Payne-Whitney Clinic. . . .

. . . I counted the tiers of metal-framed windows, and in their place I imagined . . . a wall bedizened with sparkling new tessalation, thousands of molasses-golden lions rampant on blue tiles. In my mind the tiles were as blue as sky, yet I was unable to prevent their glowing from time to time with the lurid, self-advertising, chlorinated blue-green of an indoor swimming pool. Brick by brick, and white block by block, I was myself as if building this hospital like a child.[5]

Throughout his career, Lowell would build his poetry out of just such an interplay between the conscious and the unconscious, using free association not necessarily with any specific intention, but rather because, as the prose pieces and the letter to Santayana demonstrate, it was natural for him to think in this way. Meanwhile, other poets were using free association more self-consciously. Lowell wrote his letter to Santayana before the poet's notable reading tour in California, when he was exposed to Allen Ginsberg and other members of the Beat school. Unlike Lowell, these poets used free association as a deliberate means of writing poetry; indeed, according to Deanna Silberman, "Ginsberg's theory of composition . . . is built on the Freudian idea of revealing the unconscious self through the technique of association."[6] Ginsberg names Blake and Whitman among his predecessors, but the "biggest influence," he said, was "Kerouac's prose."[7] Jack Kerouac's prose, with its echoes of William Carlos Williams, both describes and at times demonstrates a technique based not on " 'selectivity' of expression but following free deviation (association) of mind."[8] This method of writing relies heavily upon habits of mind of the sort that Lowell reveals in his prose pieces and in his letter, upon a willingness to concentrate on the yellow dog and to follow it, to begin, in Kerouac's inimitable words, "not from preconceived idea of what to say about image but from jewel center of interest in subject of image at *moment* of writing, and write outwards swimming in sea of language to peripheral release and exhaustion."[9]

The Beat poets were not the only writers who deliberately and self-consciously focused their attention on psychoanalytic methods such as free association. Surrealism may be said to have begun with this experience of André Breton:

It was in 1919, in complete solitude and at the approach of sleep, that my attention was arrested by sentences, more or less complete, which became perceptible to my mind without my being able to discover (even by meticulous analysis) any possible previous volitional effort. One evening in particular, as I was about to fall asleep, I became aware of a sentence articulated clearly. . . . I am unable at this distance to remember the exact sentence, but it ran something like this: "A man is cut in half by the window." What made it clearer was the fact that it was accompanied by a feeble visual representation of a man in the process of walking, but cloven, at half his height, by a window perpendicular to the axis of his body. . . . Preoccupied as I still was with Freud, and familiar with his methods of investigation, which I had practiced occasionally on the sick during the war, I resolved to obtain for myself what one seeks to obtain from patients, namely a monologue poured out as rapidly as possible, over which the subject's critical faculty has no control—the subject himself throwing reticence to the winds—and which as much as possible represents "spoken thought."[10]

Freud says that in the freely associating subject we see "the establishment of a psychical state which, in its distribution of psychical energy . . . bears some analogy to the state before falling asleep."[11] The reader will have noticed that Breton, like Lowell in his letter to Santayana, is reporting an occurrence that took place as he was on the verge of sleep. Both Breton and Lowell report images that spring into the mind unbidden, and both commit themselves to following the image along the path of associations. This experience led Breton to define surrealism in 1924 as the "dictation of thought in the absence of all control exercised by reason and outside all aesthetic or moral preoccupations"; surrealism "rests in the belief in the superior reality of certain forms of association neglected heretofore"—which is to say, in free association rather than reason or logic. And the aim of surrealism is to unite exterior reality with that interior reality that we apprehend through free association.[12]

It would not be quite correct to call Lowell a surrealist; he was a careful craftsman and a tireless, even obsessive reviser, whereas the surrealists prided themselves on their spontaneity and made a point of not revising their work (or at least professed not to revise—one wonders whether they would sneak in a change now and then to heighten an effect). But Lowell's willingness to follow the yellow dog into his unconscious led him from time to time to write poetry that he himself described as surrealistic in the "Afterthought" to *Notebook 1967–68*:

> I lean heavily to the rational, but am devoted to surrealism. A surrealist might not say, "The man entered a house," but "The man entered a police-whistle," or . . . make some bent generalization: "Weak wills command the gods." Or more subtly, words that seem right, though loosely in touch with reason: "Saved by my anger from cruelty." Surrealism can degenerate into meaningless clinical hallucinations, or worse into rhetorical machinery, yet it is a natural way to write our fictions.

The reader of *Notebook*, particularly if she tries to read the volume as a whole rather than to browse haphazardly among the individual sonnets, may well become impatient; some of the less successful poems indeed seem to "degenerate into meaningless clinical hallucinations, or worse into rhetorical machinery." For the most part, however, whatever Lowell is doing, it seems to work. In the "Afterthought" to the revised *Notebook*, Lowell changed the word "surrealism" to "unrealism" and counterbalanced his warning about its dangers with the affirmation that "the true unreal is about something, and eats from the abundance of reality." Alan Williamson describes how the successful surrealistic poems work in *Notebook*: they "turn . . . to the unruliness of the moment, showing us how many separate strands of sensation it contains, how weirdly the mind shuttles between them and its own equally abrupt and mysterious patterns of fantasy-thought. Lowell struggles . . . to deliver the feeling, if not the literal contents, of a basic mind-flux."[13] The poems show us, in other words, how free association feels.

Consider "Long Summer 3" (*N* 25), the third in a sequence of fifteen sonnets.[14] Lowell begins by evoking in the reader the feeling of the state he describes:

> Months of it, and the inarticulate mist so thick
> we turned invisible to one another
> across the room . . .

Months of what? The preceding poem, ending with the image of a discarded boiled lobster and its "two burnt-out, pinhead, black and popping eyes," gives us no help. We are bewildered, in a fog, anxious. We are cut off from the poet, "invisible to one another / across the room" of the poem. And we are inarticulate: the words "inarticulate mist so thick" are hard to say because we falter and trip over the "s" and "t" sounds that are jammed together.

> . . . the floor, aslant, shot hulling
> through thunderheads, gun-cotton dipped in pitch,

And what now? The syntax has dissolved and the enjambment hurls us forward, but where are we?

> Salmon-glow . . .

Explosions from guns? Hell?

> Salmon-glow as the early lighted moon

Not hell, but instead a respite from anxiety: a calm, lovely moment. But it cannot last.

> Salmon-glow as the early lighted moon,
> snuffed by the malodorous and frosted murk—
> not now! . . .

Please not now. Not the anxiety, the uncertainty, the fear.

> . . . Earth's solid and the sky is light,
> yet even on the steadiest day, dead noon,
> the sun stockstill like Joshua's in midfield,
> I have to brace my hand against a wall
> to keep myself from swaying—

A moment of reflection, as the subject steps back from the pure flow of association, and rationally and coolly assesses his situation. The conclusion is not encouraging: although the physical world is stable and filled with light, the interior world threatens, and the subject totters. He is afraid. But free association is a "forced labour," and writer and reader have determined to submit themselves to it, to follow wherever the images lead.

> . . . swaying wall,
> straitjacket, hypodermic, helmeted
> doctors, one crowd, white-smocked, in panic, hit,
> stop, bury the runner on the cleated field.

Panic, indeed, as the images come so fast they blur into one another, threatening, pressing in, faster and faster, hospital, helmets, a wall of white, the quarterback about to be overwhelmed, the patient about to be subdued by force, terror, "in panic, hit, / stop." The moment and the momentum stop, the patient is knocked out, the runner is buried forever on the cleated field.

A surrealistic poem such as "Long Summer 3" has a dreamlike quality about it, and indeed it is sometimes difficult to tell a Lowell dream poem from a poem based on free association. But it is unnecessary to do so: both kinds of poems grow out of similar processes and work in similar ways. Both offer access to the unconscious and represent its truths not through reason and logic but rather through a chain of association of images. Freud, in the "Revision of the Theory of Dreams," explains how the process works in dreams:

> The latent dream thoughts are . . . transformed into a collection of sensory images and visual scenes. It is as they travel on this course that what seems to us so novel and so strange occurs to them. All the linguistic instruments by which we express the subtler relations of thought—the conjunctions and prepositions, the changes in declension and conjugation—are dropped, because there are no means of representing them; just as in a primitive language without any grammar, only the raw material of thought is expressed and abstract terms are taken back to the concrete ones that are at their basis.[15]

Freud's description of the means of representation in dreams applies as well to free association, and Lionel Trilling explains how this mode of representation is related to art—in particular, for our purposes, to poetry:

> The unconscious mind works without the syntactical conjunctions which are logic's essence. It recognizes no *because*, no *therefore*, no *but*; such ideas as similarity, agreement, and community are expressed in dreams imagistically by compressing the elements into a unity. The unconscious mind in its struggle with the conscious always turns from the general to the concrete and finds the tangible trifle more congenial than the large abstraction. Freud discovered in the very organization of the mind those mechanisms by which art makes its effects, such devices as the condensations of meaning and the displacement of accent.[16]

In dreams and in free association and in poetry, then, truth may be represented by means of a series of images. But what takes the place of the missing conjunctions? How is one image related to another? Freud explains that "in a psycho-analysis one learns to interpret propinquity in time as representing connection in subject-matter. . . . Two thoughts which occur in immediate sequence without any apparent connection are in fact part of a single unity which has yet to be discovered; in just the same way, if I write an 'a' and a 'b' in succession, they have to be pronounced as a single syllable 'ab.' "[17] The *a* and the *b*, in other words, make meaning not in themselves but in their relation to one another, in their association. By using the letters *a* and *b* as his examples, Freud has made it easy for us to see the link here to contemporary linguistic theory, according to which the sign confers meaning not in itself but through its relation to other signs. But Freud extends the concept beyond linguistics (to the extent that any concept can be extended "beyond linguistics"), quoting the poet Friedrich Schiller with approval: "Looked at in isolation, a thought may seem very trivial or very fantastic; but it may be made important by another thought that comes after it, and in conjunction with other thoughts that may seem equally absurd, it may turn out to form a most effective link."[18]

Robert Lowell, more even than the rest of us, seemed automatically to think in relational and associational terms. Jay Martin quotes one of Lowell's students as remembering how "he would describe a phrase in terms of another phrase, another poet, a group of people, a feeling, a myth, a novel, a philosophy, a country. . . . He would compare and contrast, describe."[19] And John McCormick, referring to Lowell as "a first-rate teacher who enjoys teaching," said that his method was "to circle in upon his man like a dog upon a bird; he came to Crane by way of Tate, Emerson, Dante, and Vergil."[20] In his letter to Santayana, who had apparently been having trouble reading modern poets such as Eliot and Pound, Lowell advised that "it might be profitable to go into illogical associative structures," and his advice is helpful to readers of his own poetry as well. Robert Hass, writing about "The Quaker Graveyard," has observed that "surrealism . . . is syntax: not weird images but the way the mind connects them."[21] Marjorie Perloff says that the syntactic structure of "Memories of West Street and Lepke" (LS 85) implies "that only by viewing the self in terms of its surroundings, companions, and habitual actions can the poet come to grips with the world he inhabits."[22]

Stanley Leavy, discussing Freud's comparison of psychoanalysis to archaeology, refers to the "unearthing of the artifact according to modern methods, by which its surroundings are given as much importance as the object itself," and insists that "found objects are themselves more than merely indexical; they are truly symbolic, and may be even syntactic. The arrangement of found objects may itself be interpretable as giving a statement."[23] Robert Lowell's poetry is full of "found objects," of details whose association each with the other contributes immeasurably to the effects of the poetry. His use of specific detail, of "the horrifying mortmain of / ephemera: keys, drift, sea-urchin shells" ("Harriet 2," N 21), links him to Proust and to such writers of "realism" as Tolstoy. In The Poetic Art of Robert Lowell, Marjorie Perloff has demonstrated the extent to which Life Studies fuses "the romantic mode, which projects the poet's 'I' in the act of self-discovery, and the Tolstoyan or Chekhovian mode, usually called realism." She defines this realistic mode in the terms of Roman Jakobson's distinction between metaphor and metonymy.[24] Jakobson has said that all discourse falls somewhere between the two poles of metaphor and metonymy, which he associates with fundamental unconscious mechanisms described by Freud in The Interpretation of Dreams. Jakobson associates poetry primarily with metaphor, and prose with metonymy, which is based on the principle of contiguity. "Following the path of contiguous relationships, the realist author metonymically digresses from the plot to the atmosphere and from the character to the setting in place and time."[25]

Lowell uses metonymy often and effectively in his poems, and as he "metonymically digresses" he does something very much like what happens in free association. Jack Kerouac, whose Beat manifesto was based on the principles of free association, announced as the first of his Essentials of Spontaneous Prose the following: "SET-UP. The object is set before the mind, either in reality, as in sketching (before a landscape or teacup or old face) or is set in the memory wherein it becomes the sketching from memory of a definite image-object."[26] But the object itself is only the beginning: its importance lies in where it leads. The psychoanalyst Theodor Reik, after describing an example of his own free association, makes this comment: "These are my thoughts as I should tell them to a person in the room to whom I have to report them the moment they occur. It is clear that most of them are determined by the objects I see; the connections between them seem to be made only by the sight of the objects and by thoughts of the persons they remind me of."[27]

Lowell's poems abound in examples of this sort of process. An oak ceiling leads to thoughts of middle age, of Shelley, and ignominy ("The Golden Middle," N 131); and "Cousin Belle's half-sofa" and the "small portrait of Cousin Cassie" evoke both his childhood and the more recent past in "Off Central Park" (DBD 44). In "Myopia: a Night" (FTUD 31), Lowell is explicit about the role of visible objects in setting off a flow of associations. This poem, like "Eye and Tooth" (FTUD 18), is based on an extended pun on "I" and "eye," and Lowell makes clear the fact that what the eye sees may well lead one to investigate what the I feels. He begins the poem in that state of consciousness that we remember as one particularly conducive to free association: the state just before falling asleep.

> Bed, glasses off, and all's
> ramshackle, streaky, weird
> for the near-sighted, just
> a foot away.
>   The light's

> still on an instant. Here
> are the blurred titles, here
> the books are blue hills, browns,
> greens, fields, or color.
>   This
> is the departure strip,
> the dream-road. Whoever built it
> left numbers, words and arrows.
> He had to leave in a hurry.

For this myopic poet, the blur of books dissolves into a country scene of hills and fields, a rural airport runway perhaps, "the departure strip, / the dream-road" that he must travel, complete with "numbers, words and arrows" to point the way. Where does the road lead? As Stephen Yenser suggests, it leads directly to the study in which Lowell wrote his poems as a young man.[28]

> I see
> a dull and alien room,
> my cell of learning,
> white, brightened by white pipes,
> ramrods of steam . . .   [Lowell's ellipsis]

He sees the room clearly: the pipes, the steam; and the sight evokes the memory of a sound:

> . . . I hear
> the lonely metal breathe
> and gurgle like the sick.

This sound is unpleasant; this memory is going to be too painful, and for once Lowell turns back and refuses to follow the path of associations.

> And yet my eyes avoid
> that room. No need to see.
> No need to know I hoped
> its blank, foregoing whiteness
> would burn away the blur,
> as my five senses clenched

their teeth, thought stitched to thought,
as through a needle's eye . . .

                                       [Lowell's ellipsis]

Here past and present merge as the poet tries to shut out the memory of that "blank, foregoing whiteness" that he hoped might "burn away the blur" of approaching mania, that terrible condition in which the mind is bombarded by more sensation than it can accommodate, when associations succeed one another so quickly and so intensely that the mind feels stretched to the breaking point, painfully drawn out as though forced through the tiny aperture of a needle's eye.

I see the morning star.

Here, in a bedroom, looking through a window, he sees a star, the morning star: Lucifer, before the Fall.

Think of him in the Garden,
that seed of wisdom, Eve's
seducer, stuffed with man's
corruption, stuffed with triumph:
Satan triumphant in
the Garden! In a moment,
all that blinding brightness
changed into a serpent,
lay grovelling on its gut.

Satan is larger than life, like a young poet whose works have been roundly applauded, or like a manic patient proud of his sexual prowess, "stuffed" with man's corruption and with triumph, imbued with "blinding brightness" that never lasts, that always turns, "in a moment," into dust. And here? Now?

What has disturbed this household?
Only a foot away,
the familiar faces blur.
At fifty we're so fragile,
a feather . . .

                                       [Lowell's ellipsis]

Past and present, people and things, sickness and health, life and death, all combine and coexist. As Lowell's many ellipses demonstrate, thoughts fade in and out, come and go. "We're so fragile." But, at least for now, we survive:

> The things of the eye are done.
> On the illuminated black dial,
> green ciphers of a new moon—
> *one, two, three, four, five, six!*
> I breathe and cannot sleep.
> Then morning comes,
> saying, "This was a night."

In a poem like "Myopia: a Night," Lowell manages to convey the feeling of the experience of free association that he is describing. But in many of his "confessional" poems, and particularly in *Life Studies*, the tone seems peculiarly detached rather than involved. Alan Williamson points out that "in terms of the surrealists' ideal of a direct rendition of the flow of thought, conscious and unconscious, *Lord Weary's Castle* often succeeds brilliantly, where the later, 'confessional' writing often chooses to view psychological processes more remotely, in rational afterthought."[29] Robert Hass, writing about "The Quaker Graveyard in Nantucket," elaborates on this paradox:

> I still find myself blinking incredulously when I read . . . that those early poems "clearly reflect the dictates of the new criticism," while the later ones are "less consciously wrought and extremely intimate." This is the view in which it is "more intimate" and "less conscious" to say "my mind's not right" than to imagine the moment when
>
> > The death-lance churns into the sanctuary, tears
> > The gun-blue swingle, heaving like a flail,
> > An [*sic*] hacks the coiling life out . . .
>
> which is to get things appallingly wrong.[30]

A poem like "The Quaker Graveyard" is more "intimate" than many of the *Life Studies* poems in part because the speaker seems to have immersed himself in a flow of association rather than to have arranged images according to an aesthetic or rational order—and this despite the fact that the early poems are more formal, bound by traditional meter and rhyme.

Williamson argues that "iambic meters and rhyme, in Lowell, tend to produce, not neat rational statements, but a kind of trance," and he mentions the "intensity" with which symbols "arrive" in such poetry.[31] The images in the early poems are charged with an energy that is often lacking in the poems of *Life Studies*. Compare, for example, images from "Mother and Son," in *Lord Weary's Castle* (47), with images from "My Last Afternoon with Uncle Devereux Winslow" (*LS* 59). The poet begins "Mother and Son" with a matter-of-fact statement describing the plight of an adult male still in thrall to his mother: "Meeting his mother makes him lose ten years, / Or is it twenty?" He is a boy again.

> . . . It is honest to hold fast
> Merely to what one sees with one's own eyes
> When the red velvet curves and haunches rise
> To blot him from the pretty driftwood fire's
> Façade of welcome. . . .

The red velvet curves and haunches are simultaneously seductive and repellent; the image intervenes between the boy and the fire that promises but cannot deliver light and warmth. "Nothing shames / Him more than this uncoiling, counterfeit / Body presented as an idol"—and then, another terrible image:

> . . . It
> Is something in a circus, big as life,
> The painted dragon, a mother and a wife
> With flat glass eyes pushed at him on a stick;
> The human mover crawls to make them click.

A familiar child's push-toy appears to him as something gigantic and grotesque, and the implacable stresses in the penultimate line reinforce the threatening effect of the "flat glass eyes," pushing toward him.

With these images, effective and frightening, compare two from "Uncle Devereux Winslow," in which the poet recalls impressions of himself as a small boy, "five and a half," spending an afternoon at the family farm with his uncle, who "was dying of the incurable Hodgkin's disease."

> No one had died there in my lifetime . . .
> Only Cinder, our Scottie puppy
> paralysed from gobbling toads.
> I sat mixing black earth and lime.   [Lowell's ellipsis]

Here the adult speaker is not involved, not, to borrow Hass's phrase, "in the picture"; the paralyzed dog seems almost comic, evoking no emotion either in the reader or in the small boy who sits mixing earth and lime. At the very end of the poem, Lowell returns to the image of the boy:

> My hands were warm, then cool, on the piles
> of earth and lime,
> a black pile and a white pile . . . .
> Come winter,
> Uncle Devereux would blend to the one color. [Lowell's ellipsis]

We apprehend no intensity here, no element of submission to the flux of free association.

How are we to understand this curious detachment that pervades much of *Life Studies*? Lawrence Kramer suggests that "Lowell's style in *Life Studies* gives the impression of a discourse that is struggling with some success to obey Freud's 'fundamental rule'— the rule that asks the analysand to relax his educated impulses to impose logical, narrative or moral shape on his experience." The only trouble, says Kramer, "is that the cost of this, for the speaker, is a determined disavowal of the emotions attached to the material he brings forth." Kramer reminds us of Lowell's commitment, in *Life Studies*, to "the figure of metonymy, a trope that is equivalent to displacement in psychoanalytic discourse." He contends that "Lowell's deadly accurate representation of the props and detritus of three intertwined life histories is also a constant evasion of the emotional meaning and therefore the unconscious influence of those histories."[32] The reader may find it ironic that Lowell's conscientious attempts to dredge up important memories—a process begun at the suggestion of his psychiatrists—apparently resulted in blocking rather than opening up access to the feelings evoked by the memories.

In the introductory chapter we have discussed the splitting of the ego in psychoanalysis into two parts, a rational, observing half whose job it is to oversee and to comment on the experiencing half as the latter freely associates. By applying this concept to *Life Studies* and Lowell's other poetry we can see that some of the poetry evokes the rational, observing part of the self, whereas other poems evoke the freely associating part. Williamson says that *Lord Weary's Castle* and *Life Studies* "divide Lowell's world between them, for the one has only the barest points of reference in an unmythologized reality, while the other, despite its 'confessional' content, has almost no element of recaptured mental flux or free association." The "ultimately greater achievement" after *Life Studies*, according to Williamson, is "to unify the two realms."[33] In *For the Union Dead* Lowell wrote a poem that attempts to portray a merger of the observing and the experiencing selves. Lowell himself said that in one group of poems in that volume he wrote "surrealism about [his] life."[34] He was no doubt referring, among other poems, to "The Severed Head" (52), which Steven Gould Axelrod describes as a "surrealist dream."[35]

> Shoes off and necktie, hunting the desired
> butterfly here and there without success,
> I let nostalgia drown me, I was tired
> of pencilling the darker passages,
> and let my ponderous Bible strike the floor.

The reader of this poem, like the poet, had better take off shoes and necktie and try to surrender to the flow of association; if we try to read conscientiously and to pencil the darker passages we are doomed to failure.

> My house was changing to a lost address,
> the nameplate fell like a horse-shoe from the door,
> where someone, hitting nails into a board,
> had set his scaffolding. I heard him pour
> mortar to seal the outlets, as I snored,
> watching the knobbed, brown wooden chandelier,
> slicing the silence on a single cord.

A strange thing is happening, at least to this reader. I apprehend the flow of association here—fear of loss of identity, then fear of an ominous "someone" who is walling up the room, sealing it off, imprisoning the speaker. And I am prepared to participate in this poem, to immerse myself in it as I have done in other poems of free association, but instead I am outside, watching an interesting but unreal progression of images. Lowell's effect here recalls the claustrophobic atmosphere evoked by Poe's "The Cask of Amontillado."

> . . . What
> I imagined was a spider crab, my small
> chance of surviving in this room. Its shut
> windows had sunken into solid wall.
> I nursed my last clear breath of oxygen,
> there, waiting for the chandelier to fall,
> tentacles clawing for my jugular. . . .[36]

Now "The Cask of Amontillado" effect has evolved into that of "The Pit and the Pendulum." And next, a Poe-like alter ego:

> . . . Then
> a man came toward me with a manuscript,
> scratching in last revisions with a pen
> that left no markings on the page, yet dripped
> a red ink dribble on us, as he pressed
> the little strip of plastic tubing clipped
> to feed it from his heart. His hand caressed
> my hand a moment, settled like a toad.

I am filled with admiration for the poet who created this image, this perfect representation of the alter ego of a poet who wrote and wrote and wrote and could not stop, whose writing was his life. But again, the effect is one of distance rather than of participation, and the effect continues. It is as though the poet has split himself into an observing self—the speaker—and an experiencing self—the man with the manuscript; in this way he can distance himself from the turmoil of the writing and the life.

The speaker describes the bizarre appearance of the alter ego, the way in which he "shook his page, / tore it to pieces, and began to twist / and trample on the mangle in his rage." The rage gives way to a more moderate emotion: " 'Sometimes I ask myself, if I exist,' he grumbled," and we are momentarily puzzled, because alter egos should rage or threaten, not question or grumble like ordinary people. Is there irony here, an element of self-parody? Thomas Parkinson suggests on the contrary that the question of existence is deadly serious here, that "the alter ego of the poem is the poet objectified to his terror and disgust, so that when it says 'Sometimes I ask myself, if I exist,' the result is genuine terror since the narrator's existence is entirely dependent on that of the alter ego."[37] In any event, the moment does not last long.

> . . . I saw a sheet of glass
> had fallen inches from us, and just missed
> halving our bodies, and behind it grass-
> green water flushed the glass, and fast fish stirred
> and panted, ocean butterflies. A mass
> of shadows followed them like moths, and blurred
> tentacles, thirsting for a drop of life,
> panted with calm inertia. . . .

The sheet of glass, like André Breton's image of "a man in the process of walking, but cloven, at half his height, by a window perpendicular to the axis of his body," conveys a sense of radical self-division. And the grass-green water, the fast fish, the ocean butterflies and the shadows and the tentacles all remind us of the submarine world of the unconscious that we have discussed earlier in this chapter. Perhaps this association of the self-divided man with the grass-green waters of the unconscious can help us with the next puzzling lines of this puzzling poem.

> . . . Then I heard
> my friend unclasp a rusty pocket-knife.
> He cut out squares of paper, made a stack,
> and formed the figure of his former wife:
> Square head, square feet, square hands,
>   square breasts, square back.

Here the speaker's tone is at its most detached, indicating perhaps the poet's attempts to distance himself from the emotions associated with the activity of the artist who is brutally, "with a rusty pocket-knife," turning the person of a former wife into a distorted and severely formal sculpture—a sculpture formed out of stacks of paper.

But now the poet banishes the alter ego, and now, too, the poem begins to impinge more forcefully upon the reader.

> He left me. When the light began to fail
> I read my Bible till the page turned black.
> The pitying, brute, doughlike face of Jael
> watched me with sad inertia, as I read—
> Jael hammering and hammering her nail
> through Sisera's idolatrous, nailed head.

Like the speaker in the poem, the reader here begins to feel more acutely the emotional impact of what is being read: the page turns black, as the words themselves give way to images and vicarious sensations. The pentameter and rhyme have had a cumulative effect, and the appearance of Jael reminds us of the murderous Clytemnestras and Judiths who abound in Lowell's poetry. But the most important factor in the power of this passage is the unification, in these lines, of the two parts of the poet's psyche; rather than distancing himself from the experiencing self, the poet here achieves a hard-won union of the two. Such a union is dangerous, however. What if one fails to distance oneself from the brutal parts of one's psyche, and cannot bear the resulting self-awareness? Perhaps, like the Robert Lowell who in his manic phases sometimes assumed the identity of a Hitler or a Napoleon, one loses all individual identity in the identification with another: here not the murderous Jael, but the doomed Sisera:

> Her folded dress lay underneath my head.

The force of the line is chilling.

In a letter to Allen Tate in October of 1964, Lowell wrote:

> Thanks for liking what you like, and for being pointed and generous as always. Nothing could please me more than your

picking the Severed Head. For years after reading your terza rima poems, I've wanted to try the meter. I've always found I could not even make sense, and somehow lacked the energy to bend the rhymes to anything. When I finally did, it nearly killed me. The poem owes a lot to you in general, Wolves, the Autumn section of Seasons and elsewhere. I wanted to dedicate it to you, but thought it dull and monotonous in comparison with your much stronger and more original Swimmers.[38]

Although we might not agree with Lowell's judgment that "The Severed Head" is "dull and monotonous," nevertheless the poem seems not quite successful in its evocation of the observing and the experiencing parts of the self. In the later "Suicide" (*DBD* 15), a poem with affinities to both "Myopia: a Night" and "The Severed Head," the poet uses a different strategy. The poem begins, as do so many associative poems, at night.

> You only come in the tormenting
> hallucinations of the night,
> when my sleeping, prophetic mind
> experiences things
> that have not happened yet.

Although this speaker is describing the appearance of a frightening apparition, the voice is discursive, almost matter-of-fact: the observing self is coolly watching while the experiencing self sleeps. But the next four stanzas, set off by italics, embody a different and more intense voice, and we understand at once that the experiencing self is speaking.

> *Sometimes in dreams*
> *my hair came out in tufts*
> *from my scalp,*
> *I saw it lying there*
> *loose on my pillow like flax.*

> *Sometimes in dreams*
> *my teeth got loose in my mouth . . .*
> *Tinker, Tailor, Sailor, Sailor—*
> *they were cherrystones,*
> *as I spit them out.*

[Lowell's ellipsis]

The disintegration of the self is deeply felt here; even without the italics we would participate in the intensity of the horror. And the next stanza, although it begins discursively, quickly enters a hallucinatory state.

> *I will not come again to you,*
> *and risk the help I fled—*
> *the doctors and darkness and dogs,*
> *the hide and seek for me—*
> *"Cuckoo, cuckoo. Here I am . . ."*   [Lowell's ellipsis]

But the next stanza, although linked to the preceding three by italics, seems to return to a more detached tone, and we wonder whether this stanza is simply less successful than the others, whether without the italics we would apprehend great intensity here.

> *If I had lived*
> *and could have forgotten*
> *that eventually it had to happen,*
> *even to children—*
> *it would have been otherwise.*

The tone is musing, perhaps even despairing, but the speaker seems to be commenting on rather than undergoing a lived experience.

In any event, these thoughts of death and disintegration dissolve with daylight, and the poem reverts to standard type. "One light, two lights, three— / it's day, no light is needed." Like the situation at the end of "Myopia: a Night," the daylight brings relief but not exhilaration.

> I go to the window
> and even open it wide—
> five floors down, the trees are bushes and weeds,
> too contemptible and small
> to delay a sparrow's fall.

Or a person's, we think. The tone as well as the imagery here is one familiar from such earlier poems as "Home after Three

Months Away" (*LS* 83): "Recuperating, I neither spin nor toil. / Three stories down below, / a choreman tends our coffin's length of soil, / . . . / Just twelve months ago, / these flowers were pedigreed / imported Dutchmen; now no one need / distinguish them from weed."[39]

This exhausted tone manages to convey the impression that here the two parts of the self are conjoined, but in the next stanza, italics alert us to a reappearance of the experiencing self, and thus to the fact of self-division.

Why haven't you followed me here,
as you followed me everywhere else?
You cannot do it
with vague fatality
or muffled but lethal sighs.

Here the experiencing self directly confronts the figure of suicide, and the tone is combative, almost contemptuous. And now the detached, musing part of the self takes over to finish the poem. The italics are gone.

Do I deserve credit
for not having tried suicide—
or am I afraid
the exotic act
will make me blunder,

not knowing error
is remedied by practice,
as our first home-photographs,
headless, half-headed, tilting
extinguished by a flashbulb?

At the end of "Suicide," the figures in the photograph are headless, only parts of selves, and the poetry is equally disjointed; the associational process will not always yield a coherent narrative. In a poem that he wrote for Elizabeth Bishop ("For Elizabeth Bishop 4," *H* 198), Lowell created an image to stand for the poet on his sometimes unsuccessful journey through the poem:

Have you seen an inchworm crawl on a leaf,
cling to the very end, revolve in air,
feeling for something to reach to something? Do
you still hang your words in air, ten years
unfinished, glued to your notice board, with gaps
or empties for the unimaginable phrase—
unerring Muse who makes the casual perfect?

Unlike Walt Whitman, who had faith that the "filament, filament,
filament" ceaselessly launched out of his noiseless patient spider
would finally "catch somewhere," Lowell has no such assurance;
he envisions the poet, like the inchworm, "feeling for something
to reach to something."

Lowell's dilemma reminds us that there is necessarily a conflict
between free association, with its commitment to randomness,
and narrative. In the last chapter of this book, we will explore at
some length the tension in Lowell's poetry between the urge "to
give [his] simple autobiography a plot" ("Unwanted," *DBD* 121)
and the conflicting impulse to make poetry out of the fragmentary
and discontinuous; for the purposes of this chapter, however, we
can confine ourselves to noticing the fact that the images that bub-
ble up out of Lowell's free association do not always yield poetry
that tells a story. Discussing *Day by Day*, George McFadden sug-
gests that Lowell's "images . . . are recurrent and interrelated
in such ways as to give them a special sense or combination of
senses. They acquire additional values, especially the value of
creating links of feeling and insight with the poems that come be-
fore and after in the volume where they originate." Such poems,
McFadden says, require a new kind of critical reading.[40]

Let us consider, then, a recurrent image in Lowell's poetry—
looking not at what the image might "mean" in a particular poem,
but rather at what we might learn from its association with other
images, just as a freely associating subject might seek the meaning
of a recurrent image not in isolation but in the company it keeps.
The image is that of a turtle, and it appears first in *For the Union
Dead*, in "The Neo-Classical Urn" (47).

I rub my head and find a turtle shell
stuck on a pole,
each hair electrical

with charges, and the juice alive
with ferment. Bubbles drive
the motor, always purposeful . . .
Poor head!   [Lowell's ellipsis]

The poet's own head reminds him of a turtle shell, which contains
and confines within it the turmoil of ceaseless energy: poor head!
He feels pity for his own manic self, now and in the past. "How its
skinny shell once hummed, / as I sprinted down the colonnade /of
bleaching pines . . . Rest! / I could not rest." He remembers how
he ran past the "cast stone statue of a nymph, / her soaring arm-
pits and her one bare breast," and finally "stooped to snatch / the
painted turtles on dead logs."

In that season of joy,
my turtle catch
was thirty-three
dropped splashing in our garden urn,
like money in the bank,
the plop and splash
of turtle on turtle,
fed raw gobs of hash . . .   [Lowell's ellipsis]

Childhood cruelty, and a curious apostrophe:

Oh neo-classical white urn, Oh nymph,
Oh lute! The boy was pitiless who strummed
their elegy,
for as the month wore on,
the turtles rose,
and popped up dead on the stale scummed
surface—limp wrinkled heads and legs withdrawn
in pain . . .
  .   .   .   .
. . . Turtles! I rub my skull,
that turtle shell,
and breathe their dying smell,
still watch their crippled last survivors pass,
and hobble humpbacked through the grizzled grass.

The poet identifies not only with the pitiless boy who made music out of the turtles' suffering, but also with the tormented victims in whose pain he finds a reflection of his own.

Lowell was to repeat the association of the turtle with pain and torment in poems throughout his life. In "The Opposite House" (*NTO* 30), the poet looks out his window at the house across the street and sees a "stringy policeman," who is "crooked / in the doorway, one hand on his revolver":

> . . . A red light
> whirls on the roof of an armed car,
> plodding slower than a turtle.
> Deterrent terror!
> *Viva la muerte!*

The turtle appears in an equally unpleasant context in "Long Summer 4" (*N* 25): the image of the "turtle the deft hand tips on its back with a stick" acts to evoke the feeling of helplessness associated with the turtles dropped into the neoclassical urn, and Lowell in this poem accepts responsibility for all his acts of cruelty, for "all the ill I do and will"—a wonderful pun. The association of the turtle with guilt and terror reaches its apex in "Turtle," in *Day by Day* (98), in which the speaker, remembering his earlier cruelty, gives the hapless turtles their revenge: "in the rerun, / the snapper holds on till sunset— / . . . / as it claws away pieces of my flesh / to make me small enough to swallow."

But in other poems Lowell links the turtle not only to cruelty and helplessness but also to creativity and poetry, to love and affection, to wife and child. Lowell included "Bringing a Turtle Home" and "Returning Turtle" (*N* 242) in a small group of poems he recorded for Harvard, and it is easy to see why he liked them. The tone is one of calm affection, first established when Lowell announces on the taped recording that the poems grew out of a trip that he took with his daughter Harriet.[41]

> On a torrent highway, we spotted a domed stone,
> a painted turtle turned to stone by fear.
> I picked it up. The turtle had come a long walk,
> 200 millenia [*sic*] understudy to dinosaurs,

Those nasals . . . they woo us. Spring. Not theirs. Not mine.
A large pileated bird flies up,
dropping excretions like a frightened snake,
its Easter feathers; its earwax-yellow spoonbill
angrily hitting from side to side to blaze
a broad passage through the Great Northern Jungle—
the lizard tyrants were killed to a man by this bird,
man's forerunner. . . .   [first two ellipses Lowell's]

Much like the yellow dog at the beginning of this chapter, this
large pileated bird blazes "a broad passage" through which the
poet can follow:

 . . . I pick up stones, and hope
to snatch its crest, its crown, at last, and cross
the perilous passage, sound in mind and body . . .

Only by following the bird, with its earwax-yellow spoonbill, can
he cross "the perilous passage" and emerge, "sound in mind and
body," able to write a passage of his own about the journey to be
gone through between the beginning and the end of the poem
and the life.

often reaching the passage, seeing my thoughts
stream on the water, as if I were cleaning fish.   ["Bird," N 99]

2

A Poetry of Repetition

ALTHOUGH THIS BOOK divides the process of self-examination in general and psychoanalysis in particular into subprocesses for the purpose of discussion, each specific technique is intimately related to and in fact at some points indistinguishable from each of the others. The process of free association, for example, leads inevitably to repetition, and Lowell's uses of repetition were complex and various. Freud himself never reconciled the two mutually exclusive views he maintained with respect to the function of repetition in psychoanalysis and in life. He saw repetition both as a terrible compulsion that drives many people to reenact painful experiences over and over again, and also as a therapeutic "working-through" by means of which we can make sense of and come to terms with our experience. Lowell, too, seems in his poetry to have used repetition in similarly diverse ways. Freud began his series of conflicting statements in "Remembering, Repeating and Working-Through," where he discussed for the first time what he described as a "compulsion to repeat" that afflicted each one of his psychoanalytic patients: confronted with a demand by the doctor that he dredge up memories from the past, the patient "does not *remember* anything of what he has forgotten and repressed, but *acts* it out. He reproduces it not as a memory but as an action; he *repeats* it, without, of course, knowing that he is repeating it."[1] For instance, Freud observed, "The patient does not say that he used to be defiant and critical towards his parents'

In his fine essay on "The Quaker Graveyard in Nantucket," Robert Hass discusses "this hopelessly repeated unravelling into violence" that "is both the poem's theme and the source of its momentum. Hell is repetition, and the structure of anger is repetition."[12] For Lowell, because of the cycles of his manic-depressive illness, hell was indeed repetition. John Berryman, who knew a thing or two about mental illness himself, speculated that Lowell's famous "Skunk Hour" (LS 89) was about "the approach of a crisis of mental disorder for the 'I' of the poem," and pointed out that "one of the poem's desperate points is [the skunks'] *cyclical* approach, each night; as episodes of mental illness are feared to recur." The "Hour," he said, is *"nightly,* expanding again into a dreaded recurrence."[13] And despite his admiration for the marauding skunks, Lowell admitted that "Berryman comes too close for comfort" in his analysis of the poem.[14]

The poet Robert Lowell, who concurred in his friend's perception of "Skunk Hour" as a poem based on a "dreaded recurrence," incorporated a similar kind of recurrence in the process of writing his poetry. Another friend, Stanley Kunitz, once said that Lowell was "a revisionist by nature . . . forever tinkering with his old lines, rewriting his old poems, revamping his syntax and periodically reordering his existence."[15] Lowell himself acknowledged his mania for that disguised form of repetition that we call revision: "Sometimes there are as many as thirty versions of one poem, and I usually make more changes between magazine publication and book publication. And even when it's in a book, I want to change it again."[16] In the final chapter of this book, we shall consider the way in which Lowell's attempts to form his memories and his poems into a coherent narrative of his life give way to a willingness to accept and sometimes even to embrace radically discontinuous visions of that life. And the incessant revision, it seems to me, is at least in part a function of the ability to accept successive rather than exclusive truths about an event—as well, of course, as the result of aesthetic considerations.[17]

But sometimes revision becomes obsession, and sometimes the changes result in inferior poetry. The lovely "Water" (FTUD 3) is written in a relaxed stanzaic form which both visually and aurally reflects the poet's mood of leisurely reminiscence. As he looks back on an experience with a woman in "a Maine lobster town," the poet realizes that his memory deceives him:

Remember? We sat on a slab of rock.
From this distance in time,
it seems the color
of iris, rotting and turning purpler,

but it was only
the usual gray rock
turning the usual green
when drenched by the sea.

He realizes further that the remembered experience itself was unsatisfying:

We wished our two souls
might return like gulls
to the rock. In the end,
the water was too cold for us.

But despite the unhappy outcome of the event itself, and despite the seemingly unpleasant knowledge of an erring memory, the poet's tone is one of tranquillity and ease.

For *Notebook* (234), Lowell revised the poem, making the incident and its circumstances more specific. In this volume, it is one of "Four Poems for Elizabeth Bishop," entitled "Water 1948," and it begins with the town name, "Stonington." By this revision he not only destroys the floating, timeless quality of the original, but he crams the words of the poem into the form of a sonnet, with the effect of destroying the relaxed, leisurely pace. Then for *History* (196), he retains all the revisions of the *Notebook* version and compounds the problem by putting most of the poem in the present tense, thus rendering his dramatized meditation on the distorting elements of memory virtually unintelligible. For the reader, the effect of reading the three poems in chronological order is one of anticlimax: the repetition seems to accomplish nothing except to render the experience itself more and more distasteful, and seriously to weaken the poetry.

Notebook and *History* contain many examples of what may appear to be obsessive repetition. The sheer number of sonnets is overwhelming and reminds the reader once again of Merrill Moore's thousands and thousands of sonnets. A poet who writes an entire book of sonnets (*Notebook 1967–68*), revises the book thoroughly not once but twice (*Notebook* and *History*), extracts certain sonnets in order to publish them in a separate volume (*For Lizzie and Harriet*), then finally writes a book made up completely of totally new sonnets (*The Dolphin*)—such a poet seems trapped, in Richard Fein's words, in "some terrible reiteration."[18] His poems, as Stanley Kunitz has said, "were like the stream of Heraclitus: you could never dip into the same poem twice."[19] This habit reminds us of Whitman, with his incessant revisions of *Leaves of Grass* (as well as Pound and the *Cantos*, and Williams and *Paterson*), and Lowell's methods of revision had something in common with Whitman's too. Both poets had a sometimes disconcerting habit of lifting words, images, whole lines, and groups of lines, and placing them intact in a new and often totally different context in another poem. This habit, with Lowell, begins very early: he lifts the image of the "sudden Bridegroom" out of a poem in his first volume of poetry ("Cistercians in Germany," *LOU*) and incorporates it in "At the Indian Killer's Grave" in his next volume (*LWC* 60). But the habit is most prevalent in the volumes of sonnets.

Consider the following progression of sonnets. "Roulette," the first poem in the "April" sequence of *Notebook 1967–68* (90), is a cynical commentary on history and politics: since the time of Plato's Republic, which "never was, / except in the sky-ether of Plato's thought," people have made futile plans for Utopias. And "still" it continues. "New establishments / will serve the people, the people people serve" (or, in other words, the system serves only those already in power). In "Dalliance" (91), the fourth poem in the sequence, the speaker is a lover caught between the attraction of the beloved and the fear of being caught at his dalliance: "this flower I take away and wear with fear; / who ever noticed?" He has deep doubts about this affair, as his literary allusions prove. "Othello never caught / Cassio reeking Desdemona's musk," he says, and refers to the "Macbeth murk of Manhattan." He sounds like the Shakespeare of the sonnets, expressing his disgust at the reluctant sexuality provoked in him by the Dark Lady. "Is it a hobby like heroin or birds?" the lover asks. Then, borrowing from *Moby-Dick*, the speaker ends with the image of himself "Set at the helm, facing a pot of coals, / the sleet and wind spinning me ninety degrees," and exhorts himself:

> I must not give me up then to the fire,
> lest it invert my fire; it blinded me;
> so did it me; there's wisdom that is woe
> but there is a woe that is madness.

The allusion to Melville here is apt. In the scene from which Lowell takes these lines, Ishmael is at the tiller of the *Pequod*. Staring into the strangely hypnotic flames of the try-works, he has become confused and turned himself around, "fronting the ship's stern" so that he almost turns the ship into the wind and causes it to capsize. "Give not thyself up, then, to fire, lest it invert thee, deaden thee; as for the time it did me," he warns the reader. "There is a wisdom that is woe; but there is a woe that is madness"—an appropriate warning, in Lowell's formulation, to a man lured by the flame of illicit love.[20] But in the *Notebook* version of "Dalliance" (152), the lover vanishes after seven lines, to be replaced by "Herman Melville," who has "dragged back to Manhattan"—but the reader has trouble understanding what Herman Melville has to do with this specific lover's unwilling attraction to a woman; the repetition of the *Moby-Dick* allusion seems to make no sense when it is attached to the person of Melville rather than to the lover.

Finally, in *History*, Lowell combines the first two-thirds of "Roulette" with the *Moby-Dick* reference at the end of "Dalliance," retaining the figure of Melville and deleting the entire poet-lover sequence in "Dalliance." The result is "The Republic" (41), a meditation on the futility of Utopian planning from Plato through the American Transcendentalists. The *Moby-Dick* allusion here acts as a subtle reminder of Melville's attacks on dreamy transcendentalists in "The Mast-Head" chapter and elsewhere in the novel. And the reader who has followed the progression of poems that ends in "The Republic" has received an object lesson in the nature of one kind of repetition: like visions of Utopia, it shows up again and again but seems to accomplish nothing.

Not all repetition, however, is self-defeating and futile. Although Freud described the terrible "compulsion to repeat" and its firm hold on the psyche, he recognized a positive aspect of repetition as well. In "Beyond the Pleasure Principle," he tells the story of a small boy who invented a game that he played repeatedly. Holding a reel tied to a piece of string, he would throw the reel over the side of his cot, uttering a sound that Freud interpreted as the German *fort*, or "gone." "He then pulled the reel out of the cot again by the string and hailed its reappearance with a joyful 'da' ['there']. This, then, was the complete game—disappearance and return." The interpretation of the game was, for Freud, "obvious": because the child is in distress whenever his mother leaves him, he compensates for the loss by "himself staging the disappearance and return of the objects within his reach." Such games come naturally to children: through their play they "make themselves master of the situation," passing over "from the passivity of the experience to the activity of the game."[21] Otto Fenichel describes a similar process in the life of an adult, when he refers to "irritations that everyone experiences after little traumata, like a sudden fright or some smaller accident. The person feels irritated for a certain time, cannot concentrate because inwardly he is still concerned about the event and has no energy free for attention in other directions. He repeats the event in his thoughts and feelings a few times—and after a short while his mental stability is re-established."[22] We are all familiar with this process; our urgent need to talk about a traumatic experience and our need to replay the scene in our thoughts are, in Fenichel's words, "attempts at a belated mastery" of the event.

Freud's discussion of the therapeutic aspect of repetition in psychoanalysis is confusing, but Edward Bibrung has attempted to clarify its use by dividing the term "repetition compulsion" into two parts: (1) "the *repetitive* or *reproductive* tendency," and (2) the "*restitutive* one." Freud "originally used the term repetition compulsion now in the one sense, sometimes in the other." What Bibrung calls the "repetitive" tendency is the negative aspect of the compulsion to repeat; it is "a property of the instinctual drives of the id." The "restitutive" tendency, on the other hand, "is a function of the ego," and, as such, results in what he calls "working-off mechanisms," those therapeutic repetitions by which we are enabled to master a previously threatening situation.[23] Although the working-off mechanisms are related to the process of "working through" that Freud discusses in "Remembering, Repeating and Working-Through," the two are not identical. Laplanche and Pontalis admit that this essay "leaves us in considerable doubt as to what Freud means exactly by working-through," since he "makes scarcely any attempt to correlate the concept of working-through with those of remembering and repeating." All the same, "it would seem that in his opinion working-through is a third term in which the other two are combined. And it is true that working-through is undoubtedly a repetition, albeit one modified by interpretation and—for this reason—liable to facilitate the subject's freeing himself from repetition mechanisms."[24]

Lowell, like many poets, uses his poetry as a means of working through, and his poetic style itself mirrors that psychoanalytic process. Consider the similarity between the following two quotations, one a description by a literary critic of Lowell's style in the early *Land of Unlikeness*, the other a description by a psychiatrist of the process of working through:

> Repetition is the basis of his style: repeated symbols . . . parallelism, formal recurrence, lack of transitions, and repeated assonantal and alliterative sound devices all suggest *astonished concentration on the same matter, taken up from different aspects.*[25]

> A chronic process of working through . . . shows the patient again and again *the same conflicts and his usual way of reacting to them, but from new angles and in new connections.*[26]

A working-through, then, is a series of repetitions with a difference. The verb "repeat" loses its sense of "to do again" and gradually becomes "to say" or "to tell." Each time the poet "repeats" the original traumatic occurrence, it loses some of its power over him, so that each repetition is slightly different from those that came before.

Stanley Leavy discusses the way this repetition works in psychoanalysis:

> the past of which I claim to be fully conscious, which therefore has undergone only the interpretation of articulation itself, may shift in its articulation in successive narrations. I use different words to tell it, and in so doing I tell a different tale. . . . It is the same event, having happened thus and so and may be subject to external confirmation as having taken place, but it is in each of the two narratives a different experience of the narrator and therefore a different past.[27]

J. Hillis Miller, eschewing psychoanalytic language, applies a similar concept of repetition-as-difference to literature in *Fiction and Repetition*, a study of several nineteenth- and twentieth-century English novels. He bases his approach on Gilles Deleuze's two alternative theories of repetition in Western culture: "Platonic" repetition "is grounded in a solid archetypal model which is untouched by the effects of repetition," whereas "the other, Nietzschean mode of repetition posits a world based on difference. Each thing, this other theory would assume, is unique, intrinsically different from every other thing. . . . It seems that X repeats Y, but in fact it does not, or at least not in the firmly anchored way of the first sort of repetition."[28] Joseph Riddell, discussing Charles Olson's poetics, gives us yet another way to think about these repetitions: "To use a favorite Olson metaphor, history is a Moebius strip, a single surface that always returns upon itself. . . . History is a single surface of successive events, like successive perceptions, that return into themselves, cross through and efface each other, repeat themselves, but always with a difference. Each repetition is an asymptote." For Olson, Riddell tells us, this perception of history—especially the history of literature—is tied in with the "Document" rather than the "Narrative" method: "for in the latter, the narrator as personal interpreter dominates the movement of the text, and governs its closure."[29]

Here we are moving into a marshy area where believers in selves and subjects and green, watery origins approach the high and dry ground of intertextuality and indeterminacy, and in the final chapter of this book we shall address some of the questions raised by this conjunction. Our concern here, of course, is with the psychological and aesthetic dimensions of these questions. J. Hillis Miller cautions his readers that the two types of repetition defined by Deleuze—modes that appear to be mutually exclusive—in fact coexist in all literature. So, too, as we separate the negative and positive aspects of repetition and apply them one at a time to literature, must we remember that, in fact, the distinction is not so simple: the passage from one to the other may be so gradual as to be undetectable.

When Robert Lowell says, in "For John Berryman I" (*H* 203), "I feel I know what you have worked through, you / know what I have worked through," he acknowledges his kinship with that other disturbed poet and sometime friend who shared Lowell's early hopes that "despondency and madness" might be cured by working through painful memories.[30] In a series of poems, Lowell works through and comes to terms with a disturbing incident of his late adolescence: the time when the young Lowell, then a student at Harvard, struck his father and knocked him down in an argument over a girl, Anne Dick, whom he wanted to marry. Despite a later apology, Lowell apparently could not forget the blow, coupling it in his mind with the "invisible / coronary" ("Charles River 5," *N* 68) that ultimately killed his father. With his usual ambivalence, Lowell felt both pride and guilt after this archetypal act of rebellion.[31]

Lowell's first treatment of this incident, "Rebellion," must be read in the context in which it appears, in *Lord Weary's Castle* (35). Throughout this volume, Lowell sounds like an Old Testament prophet, castigating his people for their transgressions and predicting imminent apocalypse. He conflates history by abolishing the distinction between past and present, equating the sins of Adam and Cain with those of his New England forebears and with the sins of the present as well. And because he tacitly adopts Max Weber's theory of the malignant bond between Calvinism and capitalism, he equates what he sees as commercial and mercantile sins with religious and historical offenses such as the massacre of King Philip and his Indians by the Puritans. The young Lowell traced his aristocratic New England lineage back to those hoary sinners whom he scolds in *Lord Weary's Castle*. In leaving Harvard for Kenyon, in joining the Roman Catholic church, and in becoming a conscientious objector in World War II, he had announced his rejection of the traditions of New England and his family; in *Lord Weary's Castle*, he acts out this youthful rebellion.

The poem "Rebellion" might well puzzle a reader accustomed only to the Lowell of *Life Studies* and later volumes. Its central act of rebellion, seemingly so well suited to an open, confessional treatment, is here presented in a vague dreamlike manner. Hugh Staples, who was writing before biographical material and other versions of the poem clarified our knowledge of the incident, calls the poem an "enigmatic nightmare-vision of patricide" which is "an expression of psychological hostility towards the father-figure as a symbol of authority."[32] Staples's description captures the tone of the poem: it is not the personal confession of an individual act of rebellion but rather a stylized formal presentation of archetypal revolt. The beginning lines, the most explicit of the poem, must be approached by way of the poems that immediately precede it in *Lord Weary's Castle*, two sonnets and a ten-line poem, all sculpted with Lowellian severity. In "Salem" and "Concord," he borrows the concept of declension from the Puritan divines who graphically bemoaned the decline in morals and accomplishments since the time of the Pilgrims. Then his denunciatory energies culminate in "Children of Light." The Pilgrims, who "planted here the Serpent's seeds of light," preceded the later Puritans, who "fenced their gardens with the Redman's bones." Now, in this wartime year, "probing searchlights probe to shock / The riotous glass houses built on rock," and "light is where the landless blood of Cain / Is burning, burning the unburied grain" (34).[33]

Confronted with all this horror, what can a person do, how must one act? He can write poetry, of course, and define the terms of the problem. Or he can rebel, and in one symbolic act take his stand against the evils of the time. "There was rebellion, father," he begins, and the words establish a tone of detached and impersonal reverie. Lowell had begun "Children of Light" with the words, "Our fathers," and the "father" of "Rebellion" seems to be another such generic term: it carries with it resonances of religion and myth as well as psychology. The word "rebellion," coming as it does after the preceding poems of religious and political corruption, seems also to be a general term that might encompass any number of specialized acts of revolt, personal or political. The clause in which it appears reinforces the unspecific nature of the word: not "I rebelled," but "There was rebellion." The reader expects, not the act of an individual son rebelling against an individual father, but a symbolic act of rebellion.[34]

The next words and lines, however, appear to counteract this assumption:

There was rebellion, father, when the mock
French windows slammed and you hove backward, rammed
Into your heirlooms, screens, a glass-cased clock,
The highboy quaking to its toes. You damned
My arm that cast your house upon your head
And broke the chimney flintlock on your skull.

Despite the use of iambic pentameter and of rhyme (the last two quoted lines are the beginning of an *abba* sequence), the enjambed lines and the irregular placement of caesuras destroy the formal, ritualistic tone that the reader might have expected to follow from the first four words. And surely no poet would place an act of purely symbolic rebellion in a room with "mock / French windows," a "glass-cased clock," and an anthropomorphized highboy; the details seem to narrow the focus of the poem to a specific action in a specific place at a specific time. Of course we need not choose one version over another, need not opt for autobiography at the expense of symbolism or vice versa. But to structure the discussion in these terms is to emphasize the pressures and oppositions within the poem: the young poet, who later will write painfully "open" poetry, is here guarded and indirect. In this first working-through of a painful memory, he is trying to hold the experience at arm's length, to generalize it and to describe it without emotion.

But the feeling he is attempting to deny, in the manner of any repressed emotion, simply becomes stronger and pushes out against the walls of the poem, threatening to break out altogether in these first lines. The verbs are violent: "slammed" and "hove" and "rammed" and "damned"; they spur the reader forward, as do the caesuras placed so near the ends of lines. The momentum, however, crashes to a halt at each "k" sound (I count twelve in six lines), and the result is an impression of frustration and tension despite the seemingly cathartic content of the words. In fact, the act of the reader in pronouncing the "k" sounds duplicates the act of the poet in trying unsuccessfully to hide his emotion: "stops" or "plosives," says John Frederick Nims, "cut off the air for a moment, let pressure build up behind the barrier of lips or tongue, then release it with a tiny explosion."[35]

The explosive quality of these first lines strikes the reader as an appropriate response to the vehement denunciations of the preceding poems: this act of rebellion will suffice to dissociate the speaker from the evils of past and present (though, as we shall see, he is not unaware of the irony attendant upon the use of violence as a corrective to violence). Of course, the speaker is striking out not only at his father, but at all the father represents; as Staples observes, "the identification of the father with the heirlooms makes it clear that the murder is a rejection of tradition as well."[36]

Staples's assumption that the act described here is a murder points up the fact that, despite the use of detail that seems to pin down the action to a specific time and place, the reader has trouble figuring out exactly what has happened in these six lines. Indeed, through the first four lines, we could easily assume that it is the father who is rebelling against an as-yet-unknown something—perhaps the materialism that resulted in heirlooms and highboys. In the fifth line we learn that the speaker's "arm" has "cast your house upon your head" (with echoes, as Stephen Yenser reminds us, of the "riotous glass houses" of "Children of Light") and "broke the chimney flintlock on your skull."[37] There is no "I struck my father" directness here, but rather a deliberate vagueness. Did the son hit the father with the flintlock (which no doubt hangs over the mantle as a reminder of Indian-killing ancestors)? Did the son push the father into the furniture with such violence that the flintlock fell on his head? To pose the questions is to point out the absurdity of trying to answer them: the poet is not confessing a specific act but rather presenting a generalized scene of rebellion.

The next lines are tied to the preceding section by Lowell's rhyme scheme, but in other respects they signal a change: the shorter lines look different on the page, the meter becomes more rhythmic and hypnotic, more formal.

> Last night the moon was full:
> I dreamed the dead
> Caught at my knees and fell:
> And it was well
> With me, my father. . . .

These lines would make a striking painting: the full moon, the pleading, contorted faces of the dying (done in reds and yellows), and the speaker (all pale blues and grays) walking serenely untouched through the turmoil and anguish. The reader adopts the speaker's perspective. All feeling of violence has been drained from the poem now: no slamming and damning, no harsh consonants, but rather a calm, fluid recital culminating in the chilling "it was well / With me, my father."

Lowell accomplishes a lot in these extraordinary lines. He achieves a detached, heartless impassivity or numbness that might be considered the negative counterpart to the equally calm and detached but beneficent Lady of Walsingham in "The Quaker Graveyard in Nantucket" (*LWC* 14). The lines "it was well / With me, my father" create an effect opposite to that of similar lines in T. S. Eliot's "Little Gidding," another poem about violence and detachment published only a few years before "Rebellion": "And all shall be well and / All manner of thing shall be well."[38] Both poets evoke detachment and stillness but to opposite ends. The "me" of Lowell's lines is no person, but a representation of humankind's insensitivity to the suffering of others; his use of "my father" ties the poem to the hypocritical churchmen of past and present who preach religion but cause war and destruction.

Again linking church and capitalism, Lowell spells out the punishment visited on these sinners, using a meter that rushes the reader along: apocalypse comes quickly. "Then / Behemoth and Leviathan / Devoured our mighty merchants. None could arm / Or put to sea." After the universal punishment has been administered, Lowell contracts the focus of the poem to his single representative speaker.

> . . . O father, on my farm
> I added field to field
> And I have sealed
> An everlasting pact
> With Dives to contract
> The world that spreads in pain.

Identified with the "mighty merchants" of the preceding lines by his greed in adding "field to field," the speaker knows that he too deserves punishment: the Westminster Confession, the statement of the Calvinist faith, warns that "Thou shalt not add house to house and field to field." This sinner has made a pact not with the devil but with Dives, the archetypal rich man often identified with that rich man at whose gates Lazarus, in the Bible story, sat and begged; the story's moral is that Lazarus will end up in heaven and the rich man in hell, and the chasm between them will be unbridgeable.

The nature of the "everlasting pact" is ambiguous: if the world is spreading "in pain," it seems that an agreement to "contract" it would result in good, but the sense of the lines requires a different interpretation. Randall Jarrell is helpful on this point when he describes *Lord Weary's Castle* in terms of the conflict between "that cake of custom in which all of us lie embedded like lungfish," and "everything that is free or open, that grows or is willing to change." Jarrell uses "Rebellion" to demonstrate "how explicitly . . . these poems formulate the world in the terms that I have used"; contrasting the lines we have discussed with the last two lines of the poem, Jarrell says: "In 'Rebellion' the son seals 'an everlasting pact / With Dives to *contract* / The world that *spreads* in pain'; but at last he rebels against his father and his father's New England commercial theocracy, and 'the world *spread* / When the clubbed flintlock broke my father's brain.' "[39] Jarrell, in other words, sees the act of rebellion, the son's violence against the father, as a liberating act that gives access to the "realm of freedom"; the rebellion acts as an antidote to the hypocrisy, corruption, and violence of past and present.

But such an interpretation, while clearly true, contains only part of the truth. The young man who writes this poem is trying to come to terms with an actual incident in his life, so it is not surprising to find the poem reflecting the ambivalence of his own feelings. The pride and sense of release he feels are inextricably bound up with a sense of guilt. Richard Fein points out the irony of the conscientious objector's use of violence against his own father.[40] Throughout the poem Lowell takes pains to identify the speaker with the forces of evil he denounces in *Lord Weary's Castle*. In his first volume of poetry, *Land of Unlikeness*, he had followed "Children of Light" (almost identical to the *Lord Weary's Castle* version) with the poem "Leviathan"; its action begins "When the ruined farmer knocked out Abel's brains." Steven Gould Axelrod has discovered that "the manuscript versions of 'Rebellion' are addressed by a Cain-figure to the 'Brother' he has murdered."[41] In the published poem, having identified the speaker as a farmer ("on my farm / I added field to field"), Lowell further associates him with Cain and his murderous act by the "pain" / "brain" rhyme at the end, which imitates the "Cain" / "grain" rhyme at the end of "Children of Light."

In "Rebellion," then, Lowell transmutes his youthful act of violence against his father into archetypal rebellion, neither wholly condoning nor wholly condemning the act. For whatever reason, he does not return to the incident in his poetry until *Notebook 1967–68* (37), more than twenty years later. By this time he has perfected his so-called confessional style, and, despite his remark that the volume "is not my diary, my confession" (159), nevertheless he describes the experience in a straightforward manner totally different from that of "Rebellion." Again we must approach the poem in its context. The "Charles River" sequence, in which the poem appears as number three of seven poems, is a microcosm of that conglomeration of sonnets called *Notebook 1967–68*. Although all these poems have fourteen lines, the meter varies considerably. Lowell says that "my meter, fourteen line unrhymed blank verse sections . . . often corrupts . . . to the freedom of prose" (160), and an assiduous reader will find more deviation from than adherence to strict blank verse. The infinite variations in meter reflect the encyclopedic range of subject matter: in the seven "Charles River" poems, Lowell refers among other things to the present, the past, his parents, his first love, M.I.T., Harvard, industrial pollution, the *Anschluss*, Nero, Christ, Claude Lorrain, miscellaneous Greeks, aquaducts and arches, a snow-yellow knife with eleven blades, and plowshares beaten down to swords. He conflates the particular and the general, the fresh and the hackneyed, the present and the past into an amalgam of poetry that ranges in quality from outstanding to awful.

In the first "Charles River" poem, Lowell sets his scene: a short-skirted girl and her long-haired escort are walking at night where the "sycamores throw shadows on the Charles"; the reader familiar with photographs of the poet in his later years immediately reads him into the character of the long-haired escort. Since Lowell spent only a short time at Harvard as a student and a much longer time teaching there part-time later in his life, the reader assumes from his reference to that Cambridge river and from his use of the present tense that the sonnet is set in the present, in the poet's adulthood. In the poem, Lowell associates the river with his own blood which, "in workaday times," flows with "overfevered zeal." But this frenzied, solitary "pounding and pumping" gives way, "tonight," to a lovely, idyllic moment of immersion in a magic river: "our blood," he says,

> . . . brings us here tonight, and ties our hands—
> if we leaned forward, and should dip a finger
> into this river's momentary black flow,
> the infinite small stars would break like fish.

Karl Malkoff says of this poem that the "stream seems to display for Lowell a consistency he himself lacks. His own coursing blood —symbol of body, animality, all that lies beneath consciousness— performs 'its variations, / its endless handspring around the single I.' "[42]

In the next poem, the poet and his lover have followed the "big town river" out into the country, to "snow-topped rural roads" that "might easily have been the world's / top." Lowell describes the setting precisely: the snow, the cold, the ski guide with "his unerring legs ten inches thick in wool"; following him, the poet; after the poet, the woman—pictured in terms that alert us to the poet's psychological state: "You trail me, / Woman, so small, if one could trust the appearance, / I might be in trouble with the law." Read in isolation, this description, with its conditional clause, seems insignificant: a man is looking at a woman who is so far away that she seems particularly small and young and vulnerable. But the mere fact of the poet's seeing her in these terms indicates some degree of hidden uncertainty about the relationship; for "might," we can read at least some element of "should."

The poem ends, then, with an element of implicit guilt, and more particularly with the two words, "the law." It is not surprising to find that the next poem begins with a reference to the poet's father, and relates an act of rebellion against that traditional figure of authority. Lowell approaches this second working-through of his act of rebellion not by way of a series of scathing denunciations of past and present corruption and violence, but rather through two lyrical expressions of sensual pleasure tinged with guilt. Lowell begins by setting up the situation:

> My father's letter to your father, saying
> tersely and much too stiffly that he knew
> you'd been going to my college rooms alone—
> I can still almost crackle that slight note in my hand.

Lowell packs a lot into these lines. He sets up his cast of charac-
ters, capturing the essence of the stuffy, repressive father, and
identifying himself as the aggrieved lover. The "you" to whom the
poem is addressed is associated, by the poem's context, with the
woman of the preceding poems, so that present and past begin to
merge. By his use of the physical object, the letter that the poet
can "still almost crackle" in his hand, Lowell adds to the impres-
sion that past and present are one: memory is a powerful, sensu-
ous process here. And the "crackle" of the letter infuses the poem
with such immediacy that the reader, even without the benefit of
knowledge gleaned from later versions of the poem, assumes that
this letter had its genesis in fact.

The next lines, by their use of detail, reinforce our sense that the
poet is describing an actual occurrence.

> I see your outraged father; you, his outraged daughter;
> myself brooding in fire and a dark quiet
> on the abandoned steps of the Harvard Fieldhouse,
> calming my hot nerves and enflaming my mind's
> nomad quicksilver by saying Lycidas—
> Then punctiliously handing the letter to my father.

The speaker, whose vivid memory sees the other actors and him-
self, arranges them for us like the characters in a play, and even
injects an element of suspense. If we did not know the ending of
this play, we would assume from these lines that the "outraged
daughter" will be the active heroine, while the self-indulgent
speaker merely sits and broods on his "mind's / nomad quicksil-
ver."

Despite the effective use of such details as the Harvard Field-
house and Lycidas, this poem is less concrete and specific than it
appears. The reader has to work to figure out how the letter got
into the speaker's hands (did the speaker's father send the letter
to the woman's father, who gave it to her, who gave it to the
speaker?); and the speaker's action in "punctiliously handing the

letter to my father," though easy to visualize, is hard to locate in space: where is this action taking place? The poet, holding this painful incident at arm's length and, as it were, watching himself reenact it, is beginning to blur the details. But the next four words are straightforward enough.

I knocked him down. He half-reclined on the carpet;
Mother called from the top of the carpeted stairs—
our glass door locking behind me, no cover; you
idling in your station wagon, no retreat.

This "confession," if such it is, seems peculiarly undramatic and anticlimactic; the energy of the poem is concentrated in the first nine lines, but rather than evoking a cathartic release of tension when the speaker knocks his father down, the poet evokes instead a feeling of increased tension and frustration. The father, "half-reclined on the carpet," is down but not out; the mother holds the high ground at the top of the stairs; the lover blocks his would-be ignominious exit. The speaker has broken through not into liberation but into a trap—"no cover," "no retreat."

The frustration continues in the next poem, the fourth of the sequence. Referring to the dates, respectively, of the incident in the preceding poem, the death of his father, and the death of his mother, the poet wonders

If the clock had stopped in 1936
for them, or again in '50 and '54—
they are not dead, and not until death parts us,
will I stop sucking my blood from their hurt.

These garbled lines, with the conditional clause never resolved, reflect the extent to which the poet's act of violence against his father has become associated in his mind with the deaths of both parents. His life and theirs, his pain and theirs will be entwined until his own death releases them all. The life his parents might have led haunts the poet, for "often the old grow still more beautiful"; and he attributes his father's death at least in part to his own act of violence. "I struck my father; later my apology / hardly scratched the surface of his invisible / coronary . . . never to be effaced" (Lowell's ellipsis). The words, "I struck my father," more formal than the purely descriptive "I knocked him down" of the preceding poem, indicate an effort by the poet to imbue the act with significance, perhaps to confess it formally and thereby absolve himself. But no such relief is forthcoming, either in these lines or in the remaining three poems of the "Charles River" sequence. Through this second working-through of that painful memory, the poet has achieved no sense of belated mastery (to use Fenichel's term), but rather deepened his feeling of conflict and guilt.

In the revisions he makes for *Notebook* (66) only a year or so later, however, Lowell begins to make his peace with this experience. The first three poems of "Charles River" survive virtually untouched; the earlier account of the time "I knocked him down" is repeated word for word: no change here, merely a repetition. But between this third poem and the fourth, Lowell inserts a new poem, the origins of which we recognize immediately:

> There was rebellion, Father, when the door slammed . . .
> front doors were glass then . . . and you hove backward
>   rammed
> into the heirlooms, screens, the sun-disk clock,
> the highboy quaking to its toes . . . father,
> I do not know how to unsay I knocked you down.
>
>   [Lowell's ellipsis]

Although these first lines echo much of the language of the earlier "Rebellion," their effect is very different. The reader of "Rebellion" read it in a context of religious and political apocalypse and apprehended the act of rebellion as an impersonal revolt against the violence and corruption of present and past. But in the *Notebook* version the reader is prepared by the preceding poems for a personal expression, a comment on the incident of the letter that the poet has just described. He is clearly addressing his own "Father" here—no religious overtones as in "Rebellion"—and the tone is casual. The ellipses produce an impression of spontaneity: "front doors were glass then" sounds like an afterthought, an explanation one might insert if one were speaking.

Addressing his father in a conversational tone, Lowell makes a crucial statement: "I do not know how to unsay I knocked you down." Not "I do not know how to take back the fact that I knocked you down," but "I do not know how to unsay"—he equates the speech with the action. By referring in this way to the speech (read: writing) rather than to the physical act that prompted the speech, Lowell is indicating his own need to work through this experience, to repeat it until he masters it; the saying will suffice to counteract the doing. We know from the context that the poet here is rebelling not against the violence and corruption of *Lord Weary's Castle*, but rather against the stifling repression he feels in the presence of his family. The next lines emphasize this closed-in feeling.

> I've breathed the seclusion of your glass-tight den,
> card laid by a card until the pack was used,
> old Helios turning the arid plants to blondes,
> woman's life sentence on each step misplaced.

The seclusion, the goldfish-bowl quality, the endless cycles of solitaire, the faded plants, the mother lying in wait to pounce on a misstep—Lowell here details the bottled-up existence he hoped to break out of through his rebellion.

Did he succeed? The next lines are problematic.

> I have blown moondust in the mouth of the rich;
> you then, further from death than I am, knew
> the student ageless in a green cloud of hash,
> her pad, three boxbeds half a foot off floor—
> far as her young breasts half a foot away.

In an "Afterthought" to *Notebook*, Lowell said that he was "devoted to unrealism" and then defined the term: "Unrealism can degenerate into meaningless clinical hallucinations or rhetorical machinery, but the true unreal is about something, and eats from the abundance of reality" (262). Although it is tempting to condemn these lines as "meaningless clinical hallucinations," perhaps, on the other hand, they are "about something." Perhaps to blow moondust in the mouth of the rich is to rebel in a gentle, whimsical manner—or perhaps it is to smoke pot, or hashish. Perhaps to smoke is in itself to rebel. Perhaps in this passage the present and the past, the near and the far, the father and the son, the student of the 1930s and the poet of the 1960s become one; and perhaps this pleasant union indicates an empathic identification, a coming to terms with the father. If such is the case, then the working-through is working.

In *History*, once again Lowell works through his rebellious act in a new context. Whereas "Rebellion" had been broadly historical and allusive, and the *Notebook* poems closely personal, the relevant poems in *History* occupy a middle ground. *History* aspires to the chronological, and the poems with which we are concerned follow a group of poems set in and entitled "1930's," and only loosely related to one another. The last of the 1930s poems, and the one immediately preceding the "Father's letter" poem, deals with sublime concerns: the permanence of nature and art and the impermanence of humankind. In this version of the "Father's letter" poem, Lowell pins down the incident by name and date: the poem is entitled "Anne Dick 1. 1936" (112). This specificity, juxtaposed as it is with the philosophical nature of the preceding poem, acts to diminish the emotional importance of the described incident. Lowell makes only minor revisions in the poem itself, toning down its dramatic quality in favor of straightforward narrative and clarifying obscure points. The tone is direct and matter-of-fact, as though the poet had mastered the experience and was accordingly free to treat it as he chose: the telling has become less an emotional and more an aesthetic undertaking.

To follow "Anne Dick 1. 1936," Lowell chooses a poem that was sixth in the *Notebook* "Charles River" sequence (fifth in the *Notebook 1967–68* version), and entitles it "Anne Dick 2. 1936." Reverting to the global perspective of the last 1930s poem, he bemoans the aridity of the present, when "the blood of our spirit dries in veins of brickdust," and ends with a reference to the "lost" Christ, "our only king without a sword, / turning the word *forgiveness* to a sword." Suddenly reducing the scope as he did before in "Anne Dick 1," he next repeats the poem—now called "Father"—"There was rebellion, Father." This time through, the italicized *forgiveness* in the last line of the preceding poem reverberates through the lines and changes the reader's perspective accordingly. "Father, forgive me / my injuries," he had said in "Middle Age" (*FTUD* 7), "as I forgive / those I / have injured!"

Again, Lowell has made few changes from the *Notebook* version, and most of those have the effect of making the poem appear less spontaneous, more polished. He changes "I do not know how to unsay I knocked you down" to the less effective "I haven't lost heart to say *I knocked you down*" (Lowell's emphasis), as though to dramatize the diminished significance both the act itself and the retelling of it have for him—since the memory has lost its power over him, he must italicize the words in order to get any impact. That the memory of his rebellious act has been neutralized and rendered harmless is evident from the poems that follow "Father." In "Mother and Father 1," Lowell changes "If the clock had stopped in 1936" to the watered-down "Though the clock half-stopped in 1936"; the dramatic "I struck my father" gives way to the matter-of-fact "I hit my father," and the resulting "invisible / coronary" seems commonplace rather than charged with importance. This conversational, matter-of-fact tone continues in the next five poems, in which Lowell makes his peace with both mother and father.

Lowell was to have an opportunity to revise these poems twice more, for *Selected Poems* and the revised edition of a year later, but he made no significant changes, merely inserting an additional poem into the sequence and returning to the *Notebook* version of "Mother and Father 1." In other poems, discussed in the next chapter, Lowell deals more fully with his relation to his parents, but from the evidence of these poems we can consider his working-through of this particular act of rebellion a success. He seems to have mastered the situation, and thus been enabled to reach a kind of rapprochement with his parents. His habit of revision— "forever tinkering with his old lines" and "rewriting his old poems"—in this case at least, served him well.

The repetitions of which we have been speaking have in most cases taken the form of a return through memory to an incident in the past, and after a number of these returns the experience often seems anticlimactic, drained of energy. Such a change does not necessarily result in inferior poetry, but it does result in a different kind of poetry—poems that are often calmer, less emotionally charged: they are the poems of a person who has reached some sort of accommodation with the events of his life. In the last chapter of this book, we shall discuss the many returns, through memory, that Lowell incorporates into all his books and especially into *Day by Day*. Bruce Kawin, in *Telling It Again and Again*, suggests a distinction between the adjectives "repetitious," which he defines as the condition "when a word, percept, or experience is

repeated with less impact at each recurrence; repeated to no par-
ticular end, out of a failure of invention or sloppiness of thought";
and "repetitive," "when a word, percept, or experience is repeated
with equal or greater force at each occurrence."[43] Without taking
on Kawin's role as aesthetic arbiter, we can nonetheless make use
of this distinction to demonstrate how the poems in *Day by Day*,
despite their sometimes cooler tone, are repetitive without being
in the least repetitious, how Lowell's repetitions enrich rather than
diminish his later poetry. Or, as Lowell says to his friend Peter
Taylor in "Our Afterlife I" (*DBD* 21):

. . . This is riches:
the eminence not to be envied,
the account
accumulating layer and angle,
face and profile,
fifty years of snapshots,
the ladder of ripening likeness.

We are things thrown in the air
alive in flight . . .
our rust the color of the chameleon.   [Lowell's ellipsis]

3

A Poetry of Relation

IN "FOR JOHN BERRYMAN I" (*H* 203), Robert Lowell addresses himself to his friend and fellow poet in these words:

> I feel I know what you have worked through, you
> know what I have worked through—we are words;
> John, we used the language as if we made it.

The community that Lowell establishes here depends partly on the existence of shared suffering, since Berryman had endured much the same sort of mental and emotional anguish as had Lowell himself. But the more profound basis of the community, its raison d'être as well as the medium through which it exists—that agency through which we as readers are also brought into the community—is, of course, the medium of language; and, as Jacques Lacan has said of the significance of speech in another context, "that this is self-evident is no excuse for our neglecting it."[1] In earlier versions of the poem (*N 1967–68* 151; *N* 255), in place of the emphatic "we are words," Lowell had used the construction "these are words," which carries with it the implication that "these are (merely) words"—useful, perhaps, but ultimately ineffectual in bridging the gap between human beings, much less in relieving the suffering of another. But "we are words" makes another poem altogether. In the Introduction we have discussed the fact that, for Lowell, poetry and self-examination are parts of the same process.

"We are words" confirms Lowell's sense of the close connection between self and language. In "Our Afterlife II" (*DBD* 23), addressed to his friend Peter Taylor, he makes much the same point:

> My thinking is talking to you—
> last night I fainted at dinner
>
> .   .   .   .
>
> The room turned upside-down,
> I was my interrupted sentence,
> a misdirection tumbled back alive
> on a low, cooling black table.

Poems like these to Berryman and Taylor remind us that when we speak of Lowell's lifelong commitment to the process of self-examination, we must not fail to consider the paradoxical and rather startling fact that his search into the most private recesses of the self is not a solitary activity, but rather one that takes place in dialogue, through language. No matter how isolated a poet working on a poem may feel, the writing of a poem, or for that matter any act of aesthetic creation, is aimed at an audience and to that extent can be conceived of as an act of community, an act of relation to someone outside the self.[2] Furthermore, at least since the time of M. L. Rosenthal's *The New Poets*, we have been accustomed to think of Lowell as a "confessional" poet, and Lowell himself has said that "there is some connection" between "confessions to one's analyst" and "a confessional poem that's a work of art."[3] Provided we do not use the term reductively, we can usefully look at much of Lowell's poetry as confessional in the sense that it implies a listener from whom something more is demanded than the mere aesthetic or emotional appreciation of an audience.[4] Jacques Lacan has helped us to understand the nature of that something more: "I identify myself in language," Lacan asserts; "the function of language is not to inform but to evoke. What I seek in speech is the response of the other."[5] In other words, we define ourselves in relation to others, and we do so through language, which, "before signifying *something*, signifies for *someone*."[6] A "person's assurance of existing can only be gained through the Other's recognition of him/her," and the same is true whether the person seeks such assurance through psychoanalysis, through poetry, or through some less structured, more informal process.[7]

D. W. Winnicott, Hans Loewald, Lacan, and many others have demonstrated the extent to which a child gradually develops its own identity through an infinite series of exchanges with others, a process that continues throughout our lives.[8] Contemporary psychoanalysts place a great deal of emphasis on this developmental process: "Many analysts . . . are coming to see the exchanges in the psychoanalytic process as the most important part of psychoanalysis, whether their interest is expressed in the continental philosophical terms of discourse with the 'other' or in terms of the transference and countertransference that Freud first described."[9] Transference is that mysterious process by which emotions from the subject's childhood are evoked by the presence of the analyst and experienced with their original intensity; Freud believed that the transference "is everywhere the true vehicle of therapeutic influence."[10] The transference can involve either positive or negative emotions (Lacan, in his inimitable manner, has said that "the positive transference is when you have a soft spot for the individual concerned . . . and the negative transference is when you have to keep your eye on him").[11] Today's analysts, however, have tended to emphasize the positive aspects of the relationship between therapist and patient.[12] The *"transference effect"* is "love," says Lacan, and he adds that to "love is, essentially, to wish to be loved."[13] We know now that love and its counterpart, the wish to be loved, derive, at least in part, from those childhood exchanges through which the child begins to develop its identity; the analytic process reproduces those same conditions. It revives the old desires as well as the old anxieties, "based as they are on infinite longings for help, caring, and love, and the existential certainty of their not being gratified."[14] Stanley Leavy explains how the process works:

> The significant elements of the past, those which dominate the significance of subsequent events, are experiences of past exchanges, interactions of desire, all of which either took place in dialogues, real or imaginary, or at very least are only recoverable as dialogues. The transference, the source of the unconscious memories recoverable in psychoanalysis, is the heir of all previous dialogues, which the analytic method actively collects.[15]

But transference, and the primacy of dialogue, are not confined to psychoanalysis. "You must not suppose," Freud cautions us, "that the phenomenon of transference . . . is *created* by psycho-analytic influence. Transference arises spontaneously in all human relationships just as it does between the patient and the physician."[16] Loewald and Lacan concur,[17] and Leavy describes how transference works in "friendly conversation":

> At the same time I must address not only this hearer person-ally before me, and presumably known to me, but also other persons associated with my hearer in my own mind. . . . they are not just lay figures who can stand for anyone at all; they are real persons—living or dead—with whom I have conversed in the past or with whom I propose to speak in the future.
>
> The upshot of this line of thinking is the realization that even the most ordinary conversation admits the presence in imagination—conscious or unconscious—of more than the two actually visible in the audible dialogue. In psychoanalytic terms, then, it is clear that transference is a property of all dialogue.[18]

Thus despite Lowell's insistence that he was never psychoanalyzed, never "suffered an emotional or intellectual transference in therapy,"[19] we are justified in looking at his poetry as a series of encounters or dialogues through which he uses the methods of psychoanalysis to search for answers to the sorts of questions one asks in psychoanalysis. In these poems, he not only seeks self-knowledge through relation with another, but through concentration on the nature of the relation itself.

Before he was ready to write the personal, confessional poetry of *Life Studies*, Lowell published *The Mills of the Kavanaughs*, a book in which the protagonist of every poem identifies himself or herself through relation to another. The aging nun in "Mother Marie Therese" (106) lives entirely through her memories of her "Mother," long ago dead at sea; the speaker in "Her Dead Brother" (104) is obsessed by incestuous love for the brother whom she has "saved" in the "ice-house" of her mind. In "David and Bathsheba in the Public Garden" (110), the identities of the two characters are so interrelated that, as Randall Jarrell says, "you can't tell David from Bathsheba without a program." He adds that "they both (like the majority of Mr. Lowell's characters) talk just like Mr. Lowell"— of which, more later.[20] Lacan has given the name "mirror stage" to that period of time when the young child is learning to define itself as an entity apart from others, with the recognition of its reflection in a mirror acting partially as symbol and partially as cause; and Lowell has David and Bathsheba lie by the pool in Boston's Public Garden, "Drinking our likeness from the water"— only one of many times he uses mirror imagery in the volume.[21]

In "Thanksgiving's Over" (*MOTK* 116), the guilt-ridden husband dreams a long dialogue between himself and his insane wife, who has died in an asylum. He dreams that "the bars / Still caged her window," which "mirrored mine: / My window's window"— leaving us to wonder who is sane, who insane, who is caged, who free? "The Fat Man in the Mirror" (after Werfel, *MOTK* 114) raises much the same sort of question:

> What's filling up the mirror? O, it is not I;
> Hair-belly like a beaver's house? An old dog's eye?
>   The forenoon was blue
>   In the mad King's zoo
> Nurse was swinging me so high, so high!

An old fat man observes himself in a mirror and as his "eye" confronts his "I," he cannot bear the identity that he recognizes there. He retreats to memories of childhood, moments of pleasure and terror that cannot be separated from one another. He "serves / Time before the mirror," and finally succumbs to a nightmare montage in which childhood longings merge with adult desire, childhood guilt with adult denial:

> Nurse, Nurse, it rises on me . . . O, it starts to roll,
> My apples, O are ashes in the meerschaum bowl . . .
>   If you'd only come,
>   If you'd only come
> Darling, if . . . The apples that I stole,
> While Nurse and I were swinging in the Old One's eye . . .
> Only a fat man with his beaver on his eye

> Only a fat man,
> Only a fat man
> Bursts the mirror. O, it is not I!   [Lowell's ellipsis]

In "Falling Asleep over the Aeneid" (*MOTK* 101), another old man seeks his identity by coming face to face with images of himself, but this old man does not shrink from what he encounters. Lowell tells us that the old man "forgets to go to morning service. He falls asleep, while reading Vergil, and dreams that he is Aeneas at the funeral of Pallas, an Italian prince." Richard Fein has pointed out the connection between Lowell and this old man "who has been puzzled all his life by a relationship to a family, a history, and a literature that honors war."[22] Initially, the old man identifies himself wholly with the great Aeneas: "I stand up and heil the thousand men, / Who carry Pallas to the bird-priest." Almost immediately he shifts his attention, and communicates intimately with the dead Pallas:

> I greet the body, lip to lip. I hold
> The sword that Dido used. It tries to speak,
> A bird with Dido's sworded breast. Its beak
> Clangs and ejaculates the Punic word
> I hear the bird-priest chirping like a bird.
> I groan a little. "Who am I, and why?"
> It asks, a boy's face, though its arrow-eye
> Is working from its socket. . . .

This enigmatic passage could stand as the epitome of what Stephen Yenser has called "Lowell's Ovidian attitude" in this poem, in which referents are ambiguous and figures and objects merge into one another.[23] Aeneas and the dead Pallas face each other, "lip to lip." Aeneas holds the "sword that Dido used," in which is reflected the face of Pallas—the "It" that "tries to speak." Its question, "Who am I, and why?" is the subject of the poem. The old man, as Aeneas, gazes at the funeral pyre; then his identity shifts again. Finally, he wakes from sleep, but not into lucid reality; instead, "Mother's great-aunt, who died when I was eight; / Stands by our parlour sabre." She admonishes the old man-child to put up his Vergil and honor the Sabbath, and immediately eighty years disappear: "It all comes back." He is present at the funeral of his Uncle Charles, a hero so glorious that Phillips Brooks and General Grant pay their respects at his coffin. But Uncle Charles is no Aeneas: "my aunt / . . . tells her English maid / To clip his yellow nostril hairs, and fold / His colors on him."

> . . . It is I. I hold
> His sword to keep from falling, for the dust
> On the stuffed birds is breathless, for the bust
> Of young Augustus weighs on Vergil's shelf:
> It scowls into my glasses at itself.

The old man, staring into the face of his long-dead uncle, sees not only his own mortality but also the identity of the self that emerges only after the excessive expectations of family and tradition have been burned away. There is wonderful ambiguity in the figure of the old man holding on to his ancestor's sword "to keep from falling," and the large public questions about war and history remain unresolved. But the old man himself, even if only for the moment, has achieved a measure of self-knowledge. The young Augustus, on the other hand, has it all ahead of him. His bust "weighs on Vergil's shelf: / It scowls into my glasses at itself."

Robert Hass has said that "all the new thinking is about loss. /In this it resembles all the old thinking."[24] Richard Fein correctly describes *The Mills of the Kavanaughs* as a book "about people who can confess and explore a loss in their lives at their leisure or in terms of some permanent setting to their lives."[25] The characters in these Browningesque poems are searching for a way to make sense out of loss, and their search is epitomized in that of Anne Kavanaugh, in the title poem. In his introductory note to "The Mills of the Kavanaughs," Lowell says that "most of the poem is a revery of her childhood and marriage, and is addressed to her dead husband," and we may read the poem in addition as Anne's extended attempt, through discourse with another, to try to understand herself.

Although she addresses herself primarily to Harry, her dead husband, Lowell sets up a relationship between Anne and another presence at the very beginning of the poem:

> The Douay Bible on the garden chair
> Facing the lady playing solitaire

> In blue-jeans and a sealskin toque from Bath
> Is *Sol*, her dummy. . . .

Hugh Staples was probably the first to point out the extent to which *The Mills of the Kavanaughs* represented Lowell's break with Roman Catholicism, and he finds it significant that the Bible here is not only a "dummy" but is "Sol," not the partner but the imaginary opponent of a person playing solitaire.[26] But during the course of the poem the adversarial relation between the two turns into a relation of cooperation and community, and although it would be both fanciful and discourteous to identify "*Sol*, her dummy" with the figure of a psychoanalyst, nevertheless the two play similar roles. Anthony Wilden, in his excellent introduction to Lacan's work, explains a concept that can be helpful to us here:

> Distinguishing the Other . . . from the other (or present counterpart) is methodologically useful. The analyst may be viewed as the (neutral) other who is constituted as the Other by the subject (who is not talking to *him*) on the basis of the original or primordial constitution of the subject by Otherness. This is why self-analysis absolutely requires another to whom the subject's discourse is apparently addressed—just as Fleiss served this function in Freud's self-analysis.[27]

We must be careful not to force a ridiculous comparison here, but it is nonetheless true that as Anne freely associates from reverie to fantasy to memory throughout this long poem, she returns again and again to the reality of the cards that she holds in her hands and the Bible that faces her across the table, and their physical presence, like that of a therapist or any friendly "other," causes her either to stop and reflect on what has gone before or to change the direction of her associations.

The structure of the poem itself reinforces our impression of interrelated subjects acting one upon the other, as Lowell gives words now to the narrator, now to Anne, in a seemingly random, conversational order. The narrator begins by describing those elements of the setting that will be important as starting points for Anne's associations. Down the hill from the garden in which she sits is "a ruined burlap mill," which will act to remind her of the

history of Harry's family: the glory of their beginnings, their com-
mercial exploitation of the environment, their cruelty to the Indi-
ans, their subsequent decline (readers of *Lord Weary's Castle* may
recognize this combination of elements from the earlier volume,
in which Lowell's own ancestors were characterized in much the
same way). Near the ruined mill stands a statue of Persephone,
who will figure largely in Anne's fantasies; Staples has pointed out
that Anne is "ambivalent in all things, and for such a divided
nature, Persephone, herself subjected to an alternating cycle of life
and death, identified with the recurring seasons, is a fitting sym-
bol."[28] (Again, the reader familiar with Lowell's biography may
think of the cycles of mania and morbid depression that had al-
ready, at the time of the writing of this poem, begun to affect the
poet.)

Near where Anne sits is her husband's grave, and it is this
physical object and the associations to which it leads that form the
bulk of the poem, and to which the poem will return at its end.

> The lady drops her cards. She kneels to furl
> Her husband's flag, and thinks his mound and stone
> Are like a buried bed. "This is the throne
> They must have willed us. Harry, not a thing
> Was missing: we were children of a king.["]

But the family declined quickly; they lost much of their land, in-
cluding the "spawning ponds" that Anne remembers vividly.

> "Love, is it trespassing to call them ours?
> They are now. Once I trespassed—picking flowers
> For keepsakes of my journey, once I bent
> Above your well, where lawn and battlement
> Were trembling, yet without a flaw to mar
> Their sweet surrender. Ripples seemed to star
> My face, the rocks, the bottom of the well.["]

In the mirrorlike surface of the well, she can see the "lawn and
battlement" clearly, but her own face—her own identity—is not
yet clear. She remembers Harry's mother, who adopted her as a
child, and an incident from childhood when she was allowed to

"lop / At pigeons with my lilliputian crop, / And pester squirrels."
(The young Lowell tortured turtles, and later wrote poems about
them.)

The narrator breaks into Anne's reverie.

> The lady sees the statues in the pool.
> She dreams and thinks, "My husband was a fool
> To run out from the Navy when disgrace
> Still wanted zeal to look him in the face."
> She wonders why her fancy makes her look
> Across the table, where the open Book
> Forgets the ease and honor of its shelf
> To tell her that her gambling with herself
> Is love of self. She pauses, drops the deck,
> And feels her husband's fingers touch her neck.
> She thinks of Daphne . . .

Within the course of a few lines, Anne "sees" and "dreams" and
"wonders" and "pauses" and "feels" and "thinks"—activities com-
mon in patients in analysis and in other people engaged in other
kinds of self-examination—and the "open Book" that is "across
the table" talks back to her.

She hears another voice.

> *The leaves, sun's yellow, listen, Love, they fall.*
> She hears her husband, and she tries to call
> Him, then remembers. Burning stubble roars
> About the garden. . . .

The burning stubble of Indian wars, of destroyed land, of Per-
sephone's hell, of her own death-in-life—this is what Anne is
struggling against, and trying to understand. She would like to be
able to write her life down in a contained and orderly fashion:

> . . . Columns fill the life
> Insurance calendar on which she scores.
> The lady laughs. She shakes her parasol.
> The table rattles, and she chews her pearled,

Once telescopic pencil, till its knife
Snaps open. "*Sol*," she whispers, laughing, "*Sol*,
If you will help me, I will win the world."

As the rest of this very long poem proves, "Sol" cannot help Anne
enough for her to "win the world." But for the reader of the poem,
no such resolution is necessary: just as much of the energy of
Robert Lowell's poetry derives from his struggle to understand
himself, so does our interest in "The Mills of the Kavanaughs"
depend upon the process of Anne's self-examination and the ex-
tent to which that process incorporates an "other."

Anne interests us too, of course, because she reminds us of
Robert Lowell. Randall Jarrell says that Anne "is first of all a sort of
symbiotic state of the poet. (You feel, 'Yes, Robert Lowell would
act like this if he were a girl'; but whoever saw a girl like Robert
Lowell?)"[29] We can see *The Mills of the Kavanaughs* as a practice
field upon which Lowell could experiment with poems about self-
examination, without having to commit himself to the personal
voice that would emerge in *Life Studies*. Wyatt Prunty says that
the "real action" of the poem is "Anne's unraveling of the meaning
of events" and adds that this "re-presenting of self, established
through the connexity [*sic*] of time, is what Lowell matures as his
method in *Life Studies*."[30] In the Introduction we discussed the
extent to which, for Lowell, poetry and self-examination are inter-
related parts of the same process. And in *Life Studies* as well as in
his other volumes, we can see that, like Anne Kavanaugh, he ad-
dresses himself to an "other" who serves a complicated combina-
tion of functions.

Richard Tillinghast reports that he once asked Lowell about the
identity of the "you" in Lowell's poem "The Lesson" (*FTUD* 15).
Lowell replied, "*You*, I've never quite known . . . I felt a tremor
of addressing someone loved, a close friend, myself, a girl."[31]
As Lacan, Leavy, and others have taught us, this indeterminate
"you" includes within it an infinite number of people—the people
through whom, as through an analyst, the poet seeks to establish
his identity. Leavy says that all the desires of a patient in analysis
are embodied in "the want for something from the analyst," and
that "whatever else this want comprises, it is a desire for full rec-
ognition—recognition of oneself as one knows oneself, and as one

does not know oneself, but hopes to know."[32] And Robert Lowell, through his poetry, seeks precisely this sort of recognition.

Sometimes this dependence of the poet on others for his own sense of identity is stifling and imprisoning:

> Somewhere a white wall faces a white wall,
> one wakes the other, the other wakes the first,
> each burning with the other's borrowed splendor—
> the walls, awake, are forced to go on talking,
> their color looks much alike, two shadings of white,
> each living in the shadow of the other.
> How fine our distinctions when we cannot choose!
> .   .   .   .
> At this point of civilisation, this point of the world,
> the only satisfactory companion we
> can imagine is death—this morning, skin lumping in my throat
> I lie here, heavily breathing, the soul of New York.
>
> ["Two Walls," H 169]

Alan Williamson calls this poem, subtitled in *History* "1968, Martin Luther King's Murder," the "emotional nadir" of *Notebook*. He sees the two walls, "forced to keep on talking," as a portrayal of among other things an unsatisfactory marriage. He also finds in the poem psychological, political, and metaphysical despair: "all definition, whether of the self or anything else, is relative (i.e., by relation). But if there are only the Two, and they never merge in the One, then all relation goes in a circle; real choice becomes impossible, and identities and values have no basis except in an infinite regression."[33] Such thinking emerges in the "chronic and eventually systematic pessimism" that Vereen Bell finds in Lowell's work, and certainly a reader can find many poems that present a grim picture of reality.[34]

But we know that, for Lowell, poetry was the means of bearing his life, of bearing reality; and, as we have seen, this process of examining the self and of writing the poetry evokes the presence of others. Ian Hamilton speaks of the "unbending intimacy between the poet and his addressee" in *Notebook*.[35] It is this intimacy, whether between Lowell and an indeterminate "you" or between the poet and a specific named person, that pervades his work. The poems in *Life Studies*, however, require that we distinguish between the "you" to whom a Lowell poem is addressed, and the "character" in the poem in relation to whom the poet identifies himself, even though the two cannot always be separated. Jay Martin describes *Life Studies* in these terms: "Reviving Henry James' concept of autobiography in *A Small Boy and Others*, [Lowell] first gives an account of the solitary 'small boy,' then of the 'others' through whom he further defines himself and grows to manhood."[36] Although Lowell concentrates in *Life Studies* on the relation between himself and important others, the intimacy of address that Hamilton sees in *Notebook* is almost wholly lacking. We have previously discussed the splitting of the poet's ego into an experiencing half and an observing half and noticed how Lowell seems sometimes "in the picture" of a poem, and at other times "outside the picture," observing and commenting on it. In *Life Studies* we encounter the observing, reasoning Lowell trying to portray and to understand the nature of his relations (in at least two senses of the word), but only occasionally allowing the experiencing self to speak out of its need for connection with and recognition by the "other."

Both Lawrence Kramer and Karl Malkoff discuss *Life Studies* in terms of what Kramer calls Lowell's "volatility of ego"—his inability to define himself in any way other than through identification with others.[37] Of course we all define ourselves through relation with others—this concept is fundamental to our discussion in this chapter. But it is also possible, as Malkoff suggests, that "Lowell rejects a simplistic view of the self, that rather than understanding it to be a relatively constant core, of which relationships with the outer world are important manifestations, he conceives of the self as inseparable from those relationships and therefore impossible to isolate as a discrete entity."[38] This perspective requires us to see that the small child Lowell was in a bad fix indeed. For him, as Jay Martin reminds us, "childhood was a set of contradictions: He idealized but feared his mother, while he depreciated but secretly admired his father. He thus developed what Erik Erikson calls a 'negative identity': He made the best of a thoroughly bad lot of possible identifications."[39]

"Mother" and "Father," of course, are, apart from Lowell himself, the main characters in *Life Studies*. The adult poet coolly describes Father, retired from the Navy and fired from his job, humming "Anchors Aweigh" in the bathtub ("Commander Lowell" 70), or mumbling "yes, yes, yes," to Mother's demands ("91 Revere Street" 19). Father himself is defined largely in relation to Mother: Lowell begins "Commander Lowell" not with a description of Father but with a paragraph devoted to Mother and her son—a characterization in itself, much like the picture in "During Fever" (79) of Mother and Son "rehashing Father's character" as he tiptoes down the stairs to chain the door. The relation between Father and Mother, who dominates the household and then "drag[s] to bed alone" to "read Menninger" ("Commander Lowell"), and the relation of each parent to the child who "used to sit through the Sunday dinners absorbing cold and anxiety from the table" ("91 Revere Street" 43), are of paramount importance to the adult poet of *Life Studies*. He knows that their relation has shaped his life and through most of the volume he keeps the emotions associated with that knowledge under tight control; he observes rather than experiences. Only after his mother's death (in the roughly chronological Part Four of this autobiographical volume) does he feel able to address her directly: "Your nurse could only speak Italian, / but after twenty minutes I could imagine your final week, / and tears ran down my cheeks." This intimacy lasts only long enough to be immediately undercut by irony: "Mother travelled first-class in the hold" in her "*Risorgimento* black and gold casket" ("Sailing Home from Rapallo," *LS* 77). The mixture of tones in these lines is effective: the moment of lived experience, of empathic identification, followed by the flash of sarcasm—naturally Charlotte Lowell, who had worried that their Revere Street home was "barely perched on the outer rim of the hub of decency" ("91 Revere Street" 15), must travel first class on her final journey across the Atlantic.

When the poet Robert Lowell addresses himself explicitly to his dead mother in a poem that he writes for an audience to read, the detached observer self gives way for a second and allows both himself and his readers to experience a flicker of emotion. We must not perceive the reader's role in these poems as passive; we are not mere overhearers of a son's poignant expression of grief. Rather, we are the "other" to whom he can express, in words, his love and anger and thereby learn better how to understand himself. And our role is the same whether the experiencing part of the poet's ego is addressing a specific "other" through us, or whether the observing part is describing and commenting and trying to understand. Audience and specific addressee merge to form an "other," a wall against which the poet can bounce his words.

In "During Fever," the poem that follows "Sailing Home from Rapallo," Lowell addresses his mother (and us) again, in another complicated combination of tone and underlying emotion:

> Mother, Mother!
> as a gemlike undergraduate,
> part criminal and yet a Phi Bete,
> I used to barge home late.
> Always by the bannister
> my milk-tooth mug of milk
> was waiting for me on a plate
> of Triskits.

This memory evokes tenderness and affection in the poet almost in spite of himself, but as in the preceding poem, the tenderness is undercut by his awareness of the implications of Mother's habitual gesture. Milk and Triskits! Even the proper name is ludicrous.

> Often with unadulterated joy,
> Mother, we bent by the fire
> rehashing Father's character—
> when he thought we were asleep,
> he'd tiptoe down the stairs
> and chain the door.

Lowell's witty use of "unadulterated joy" not only emphasizes the Oedipal component of this relationship, but also underscores the conspiratorial pride of Mother and Son, tinged as it is with guilt, pity, and contempt for Father, that necessary third party to whom they feel superior.

Lowell did not confine his concentration on the relation between himself and his parents to *Life Studies*. Chapter 2 discussed in detail the series of poems in which Lowell works through the memory of the traumatic adolescent experience of striking his father and knocking him down. These poems appear in *Lord Weary's Castle*, *Notebook 1967–68*, *Notebook*, and *History*, and other volumes include other poems in which Lowell seeks to come to terms with his parents. In "Middle Age" (*FTUD* 7), at the age of forty-five, he is terrified because he is still confronted by an "other" to whom he cannot relate: "At every corner, / I meet my Father, / my age, still alive." But he can blurt out, with typical Lowellian Christian overtones, words of entreaty:

> Father, forgive me
> my injuries,
> as I forgive
> those I
> have injured!

In *History*, linked by proximity to the poems about his adolescent rebellion, Lowell confesses anxiety about his lack of an independent sense of self: "now more than before fearing everything I do / is only (only) a mix of mother and father" ("Mother, 1972" 115). But because he has concentrated on the nature of his relation to his parents and has tried to understand it, he is able to take positive steps toward establishing his own identity, acknowledging the crucial importance of the relation but moving beyond it to encounter the parents in a relation of equality: "Mother and Father, I try to receive you / as if you were I, as if I were you, / trying to laugh at my old nerveracking jokes" ("Returning" 115).

Besides his parents, other family members were important in Lowell's life and continue to be important in his poetry. Chief among those who mediated and moderated the influence of his parents was Grandfather Winslow, "manly, comfortable, / overbearing, disproportioned" like the decor of his farmhouse ("My Last Afternoon with Uncle Devereux Winslow," *LS* 59). Although Lowell criticized the capitalist "craft / That netted you a million dollars" in "Five Years Later" (*LWC* 25), he imbued Part Four of *Life Studies* with this presence who was so important to the child Robert Lowell. "He was my Father. I was his son," Lowell says in "Dunbarton" (65). In "Grandparents" (68), "back here alone" at the old farmhouse, he gazes at the billiards-table "where Grandpa, dipping sugar for us both, / once spilled his demi-tasse." This memory becomes so intense that, for a moment, Lowell relaxes his cool concentration on the relationship of child and grandfather, and allows himself to express the emotion of the young child here repeated in the remembering adult: "Never again / to walk there, chalk our cues, / insist on shooting for us both. / Grandpa! Have me, hold me, cherish me!"

"Harriet Winslow, who owned this house, / was more to me than my mother," Lowell says in "Soft Wood" (*FTUD* 63). Although he exaggerates here, probably out of love and his acute awareness of her painful illness, we know that Lowell loved Cousin Harriet enough to name his daughter after her. And the young girl Harriet, like her father, defines herself in relation to those around her. In "Words of a Young Girl" (*N* 146), the child complains, "We met a couple, not people, / squares asking Father whether he was his name— / none ever said that I was Harriet." Gabriel Pearson says of this poem that "her father's 'name' threatens Harriet with the loss of her own; he consumes her, entirely engulfs her in his Lowell substance and leaves no space for 'Harriet' to flourish in." But paradoxically, Pearson points out, while Lowell is illustrating the dangers of losing one's individual identity in the larger identity of family, he is also authenticating Harriet as an individual—giving her a voice, "releasing her into her own first person."[40]

In this poem, the acts of being, naming, speaking, and writing cannot be separated; for Lowell, too, all these processes are inextricably intertwined. He derived not only his Lowell name but also his nickname, Cal, from others: "My namesake, Little Boots, Caligula," he begins in "Caligula" (*FTUD* 49). Like the young child who learns about his otherness by looking in a mirror, the poet peers at Caligula's likeness on a "rusty Roman Medal"; there, sneering back at him, he sees "my lowest depths of possibility." And both his being and his writing depended on incorporation of the identities and language of others. Speaking of *Life Studies*, Lawrence Kramer relates "the speaker's volatility of voice" with "his volatility of ego, which is otherwise represented by his incessant identifications. Repudiating any single voice, the speaker composes himself of many voices; and instead of adding these up into a unified persona or personality, he defines himself as the indeterminate space that envelops them, the unspeaking voice that articulates those that speak."[41]

Lowell's method of composition "was uniquely collaborative." According to his friend Stanley Kunitz, Lowell

made his friends, willy-nilly, partners in his act, by showering
them with early drafts of his poems, often so fragmentary and
shapeless that it was no great trick to suggest improvements.
Sometimes you saw a poem in half a dozen successive ver-
sions, each new version ampler and bolder than the last. You
would recognize your own suggestions embedded in the text
—a phrase here and there, a shift in the order of the lines—
and you might wonder how many other hands had been in-
volved in the process. It did not seem to matter much, for the
end product always presented itself as infallibly, unmistak-
ably Lowellian. . . . In a sense the representative voice of our
age was a collective poet.

Lowell was a "collective poet" in another sense as well, as Kunitz
relates in an anecdote. Once, when he was visiting Lowell in the
hospital (where in his manic phases, as we know, he often as-
sumed the identity of historical figures), "he read 'Lycidas' aloud
to me, in his improved version, as if to assert his proprietary stake
in the original."[42]
   Throughout his life, Lowell defined himself personally and po-
etically through his relations with writers, living and dead. In his
poem "For George Santayana" (LS 51), he articulates his sense of
the space in which being and writing, both of the living and the
dead, come together.[43]

> Old trooper, I see your child's red crayon pass,
> bleeding deletions on the galleys you hold
> under your throbbing magnifying glass,
> that worn arena, where the whirling sand
> and broken-hearted lions lick your hand
> refined by bile as yellow as a lump of gold.

In that worn arena of intertextuality, Lowell meets Santayana and
Milton, Hart Crane and Sappho. Sometimes he takes words from
them, sometimes he gives them words of his own to speak. He
talks to them and they talk back to him, and some of their most
fruitful dialogues grow into Lowell's translations or "imitations" of
others' poems. As early as Lord Weary's Castle, Lowell published
adaptations from Villon, Rimbaud, Valéry, and Rilke, and the ap-
pendix to Day by Day consists of three translations—the last few

pages of the last volume of poetry by Robert Lowell. In between, of course, comes *Imitations*. In an essay called *"Imitations*: Translation as Personal Mode," Ben Belitt says that "translation may serve the translator as a form of surrogate identity."[44] Jay Martin explains how the poet forges that identity: "In *Imitations*, a single mode of the imagination predominates: the poet confronts and understands himself through engagement with all that is not-the-self."[45]

Yet there may be danger in allowing oneself to be defined totally by others. To give too much power to the "other" is to face "the dissolution of ourselves into others, / like a wedding party approaching the window" ("The Landlord," *I* 145); and in the worn arena of the blank page the weak poet risks being bested by the stronger. But for the most part, the collaboration between Lowell and the poets of his *Imitations* is fruitful. Of course Lowell does not confine his interaction with writers to *Imitations*. *History*, in particular, abounds in conversations between Lowell and other poets and prose writers. He talks to Allen Tate, to Robert Frost, Theodore Roethke, Delmore Schwartz, Mary McCarthy, Sylvia Plath, Adrienne Rich. And many of the poets talk back to him. "Don't you loathe to be compared to your relatives?" T. S. Eliot asks ("T. S. Eliot," *H* 140). "Horizontal on a deckchair in the ward," Ezra Pound complains that, with Eliot dead, "Who's left alive to understand my jokes?" ("Ezra Pound," *H* 140). And Elizabeth Bishop, caught in "the worst situation I've ever / had to cope with," expresses her sense of the mutuality of their relationship: "That is what I feel I'm waiting for: / a faintest glimmer I am going to get out / somehow alive from this. Your last letter helped" ("For Elizabeth Bishop 3. Letter with Poems for Letter with Poems," *H* 197). Lowell's last *letter* helped Bishop; language bound these people together.

Like Elizabeth Bishop, many of the writers and artists that Lowell knew were his friends as well, and Lowell had a great capacity for friendship. A reader of Ian Hamilton's biography is struck not only by Lowell's love for his friends and his unselfconscious expressions of concern for them, but also by the tenacious loyalty with which his friends reciprocated his love. Blair Clark and Frank Parker, members with Lowell of the "mini-phalanx" devoted to "unmerciful self-scrutiny" at prep school, remained his lifelong friends, and, indeed, Blair Clark emerges as one of the heroes of

Hamilton's biography, quietly rescuing Lowell time after time from one or another complication arising from his mania. The young Lowell persuaded Parker that the latter was to be an artist, and in "To Frank Parker" (*DBD* 91) he explains the importance the two friends had for each other:

> We looked in the face of the other
> for what we were.
> Once in the common record heat
> of June in Massachusetts,
> we sat by the school pool
> talking out the soul-lit night
> and listened to the annual
> unsuffering voice of the tree frogs,
> green, aimless and wakened:
> "I want to write." "I want to paint."

When Lowell remembers the time, "forty years ago," that the two young friends "looked in the face of the other / for what we were," he is reminding us once again that people define themselves not in isolation but through others, that a "person's assurance of existing can only be gained through the Other's recognition of him/her." Friends will not leave us alone; like analysts and therapists, they demand that we ask the hard questions about our lives. Randall Jarrell, "Child Randall," comes back from the dead to appear to Lowell in a dream: "They come this path, old friends, old buffs of death. / Tonight it's Randall," asking, demanding, "tell me, / Cal, why did we live? Why do we die?" ("Randall Jarrell 2," *H* 126; "Randall Jarrell," *H* 135). Peter Taylor, too, like Jarrell a friend dating from the years at Kenyon, appears again and again in Lowell's poetry, and causes the poet to speculate on his own life and his relation to the world around him. In "Our Afterlife II" (*DBD* 23), Lowell dramatically describes how his own identity is bound up with that of his friend:

> Leaving a taxi at Victoria,
> I saw my own face
> in sharper focus and smaller
> watching me from a puddle
> or something I held—*your* face

on the cover of your *Collected Stories*
seamed with dread and smiling—

The self that Lowell sees reflected clearly in the puddle merges
into that of his friend, and Taylor's face in turn enables Lowell
to define himself, with a wonderfully ironic pun on his illness:
"old short-haired poet / of the first Depression, / now back in
currency."

At the beginning of this chapter we discussed Lowell's state-
ment in this poem that "my thinking is talking to you," and his
perception of himself as "my interrupted sentence"—both exam-
ples of Lowell's awareness of the extent to which the self is de-
fined through discourse with another. Later in the poem, still talk-
ing to Taylor, he emphasizes another aspect of relationship: "Our
loyalty to one another sticks like love . . ." (Lowell's ellipsis). We
recall Lowell's reply to Tillinghast's question about the identity of
an indeterminate "you" in a poem: "*You*, I've never quite known
. . . I felt a tremor of addressing someone loved, a close friend,
myself, a girl." And this remark, in turn, reminds us of the extent
to which Lowell, in his poetry, defines himself through relation-
ship with women. The reader of Hamilton's biography of Lowell
soon learns that one of the first indications of an incipient manic
attack was the poet's single-minded attachment to a young wom-
an. He wrote a lot of poems to and about women, including
"Mexico," a sonnet sequence in *Notebook* and *For Lizzie and Harriet*
in which he details an idyllic affair with a young woman, the two
of them "knotted together in innocence and guile" ("Mexico 2,"
N 101). Alan Williamson describes how the intensity of these
love poems, so firmly grounded in the geography and history of
Mexico, culminates in an experience of transcendence.[46] Although
we must be careful not to make a facile and false equation between
sex and self-knowledge, Lowell clearly sees this romantic inter-
lude as having important consequences for himself. In "Mexico
11" (*N* 106), toward the end of the series of poems, he moves
beyond the immediate experience in Mexico, and projects himself
into the mind of the beloved:

Those other yous, you think, are they meaningless in toto,
test-rockfalls you crudely approached and coarsely conquered,
leaving no juice in the flaw, mind lodged in mind?

Those others, those yous . . . a child wants everything—
things! A child, though earnest, is not quite mortal.

[Lowell's ellipsis]

"Those other yous"—those others whom you know (and the bibli-
cal usage works beautifully here), for good or for ill—"those oth-
ers, those yous": Lowell, through the young woman, is confirming
our sense that we are who we are through others. Further, by
merging the experience of adult sexual desire with the child's
more diffused perception ("a child wants everything"), he illus-
trates an elemental fact: in the child's wanting, and the concomi-
tant not-getting, is born adult desire. As the adult continues the
child's attempts to satisfy his desires (in the largest sense), "love
blots the categories," and the intensity of the child's emotion suf-
fuses the adult. Thus, transference. And thus, with luck, at least
the possibility of greater insight into the self.

Discussing the poems in *Notebook*, Williamson has this to say
about marriage: "[It] expresses longings that are more ultimate,
more dangerous (perhaps because, in Freudian terms, they are
more directly and openly related to the original longings of child-
hood), hence may be the true journey into the unconscious, the
true opportunity for the death and rebirth of the self." The de-
scriptions of married life in these poems, Williamson says, "are
almost unremittingly painful"; but "there is a kind of back-handed,
existential praise of marriage . . . the one encounter so unremit-
ting that it breaks down all our normal and solipsistic ways of
conceiving our relationships . . . and forces us to acknowledge the
person as beyond all our frames of reference, *an* other and *the*
Other." Whether we speak in terms of death and rebirth of the
self, of disintegration and reintegration of the ego, or in more
general terms of painful feelings that may evolve into more pleas-
ant ones, we can see that Lowell's marriage poems embrace the
entire range of possibilities and provide us with an encyclopedia
of the ways in which spouses learn about themselves through
each other.

Ambivalence imbues these poems. In "Obit" (*FLAH* 48), Lowell
talks about the death of the body, the death of love, the death of a
marriage:

Our love will not come back on fortune's wheel—
in the end it gets us. . . .

.   .   .   .

Before the final coming to rest, comes the rest
of all transcendence in a mode of being, hushing
all becoming. I'm for and with myself in my otherness,
in the eternal return of earth's fairer children,
the lily, the rose, the sun on brick at dusk,
the loved, the lover, and their fear of life,
their unconquered flux, insensate oneness, painful

                              "It was. . . ."
                                    [Lowell's ellipsis]

We can read this poem, as Williamson does, as one in which a
"darker unity succeeds in abolishing the sense of self-division into
an 'I' and an 'other.' " But in addition, it seems to me, we must
acknowledge the fact that Lowell, in this lovely poem, expresses a
sense of being "for and with myself *in my otherness*"—his own
identity as a separate individual paradoxically confirmed through
this experience of oneness with the world. The poet cannot decide
to what extent this feeling of oneness encompasses the wife: "old
wives; / I could live such a too long time with mine." He ends, as
so often, with a question: "After loving you so much, can I forget /
you for eternity, and have no other choice?"

Lowell's ambivalence about marriage continued throughout his
poetic career: his last volume of poems, *Day by Day*, begins with a
poem in which the wandering Ulysses returns home to an inacces-
sible Penelope, but closes with an adaptation from Propertius in
which the young Arethusa pleads longingly for her husband's re-
turn from war. In both that volume and *The Dolphin*, the poet is
addressing and discussing and incorporating and pondering both
Elizabeth Hardwick and Caroline Blackwood, his second and third
wives. Steven Gould Axelrod has said that in *The Dolphin*, "the
poet momentarily unites with the dolphin/Caroline/mermaid—a
numinous, multidimensional symbol of otherness (eros, muse,
text, nature, human being)." Axelrod finds "the metaphor of mar-
riage" in that volume important also, "a wedding of duality into
oneness."[47] In that volume, too, are included the poems that
caused such a furor: poems in which Lowell incorporated pas-

sages from some of Hardwick's letters to him and which some readers accordingly consider an unconscionable violation of Hardwick's privacy.

No doubt Lowell perceived the situation differently. Throughout his career, as we have noted, he adopted the words—spoken and written—of others. In his poetry he used the informal suggestions of his friends, snippets of conversation he remembered, and quotations from poems and published prose of others from Dante to Randall Jarrell. Sometimes, too, he used excerpts from letters, as he apparently did in the poem "For Elizabeth Bishop 3. Letter with Poems for Letter with Poems" that we have earlier mentioned in connection with Lowell's "uniquely collaborative" method of composition. Perhaps Lowell dignifies Hardwick by incorporating her words into his poems.

From the time she first appears in his poetry, the two of them lying in "Mother's bed" in "Man and Wife" (LS 87), he remarks on her verbal power.[48] He remembers the time in Greenwich Village when "the shrill verve / of your invective scorched the traditional South." And he closes the poem with the sound of "your old-fashioned tirade— / loving, rapid, merciless— / break[ing] like the Atlantic Ocean on my head." Words can hurt, of course—this tirade is "merciless"; each spouse will use language hurtfully, and the marriage of this man and wife will end in divorce. But by the time of Day by Day, the poet will be insisting that "our light intimacy of reference is unbroken" ("Off Central Park [For E.H.]" 44).

In "Home" (DBD 113), a harrowing poem that takes place in the poet's "home," a mental hospital, he explains more fully how important this "intimacy of reference" has been to him. The poem begins in a hell of noncommunication, a place where people talk past each other to a void.

> Our ears put us in touch with things unheard of—
> the trouble is the patients are tediously themselves,
> fussing, confiding . . . committed voluntaries,
> immune to the outsider's horror.
> The painter who burned both hands
> after trying to kill her baby, says,
> "Is there no one in Northampton
> who goes to the Continent in the winter?"
> The alcoholic convert keeps smiling,

"Thank you, Professor, for saving my life;
you taught me homosexuality is a heinous crime."
I hadn't. I am a thorazined fixture
in the immovable square-cushioned chairs
we preoccupy for seconds like migrant birds. [Lowell's ellipsis]

By the end of the poem, since he cannot find any "other" with whom to talk, he is reduced to imagining a dialogue:

I cannot sit or stand two minutes,
yet walk imagining a dialogue
between the devil and myself,
not knowing which is which or worse,
saying,
as one would instinctively say Hail Mary,
I wish I could die.
Less than ever I expect to be alive
six months from now—
1976,
a date I dare not affix to my grave.

In his despair, he grasps at a memory, and ends the poem with these crucial lines:

The Queen of Heaven, I miss her,
we were divorced. She never doubted
the divided, stricken soul
could call her Maria,
and rob the devil with a word.

"The Queen of Heaven, I miss her, / we were divorced." These are among the saddest lines in all of Lowell's poetry, expressing matter-of-factly as they do the most profound sense of alienation. The Queen of Heaven is Mary, of course, and a reference to the early enthusiastic Roman Catholicism that Lowell later professed to abandon.[49] But surely the figure of the Queen of Heaven also incorporates Lowell's wives and his mother, and all the women through whom, throughout his life, he hoped to satisfy his yearning for that recognition that would confirm him in his identity. Such a recognition must come, of course, through language: that lost and mourned-for Queen of Heaven "never doubted / the divided, stricken soul" could "rob the devil with a word," with his many words, with his poetry.

Reviewing Eliot's "Four Quartets" in 1943, Lowell remarked that his "own feeling is that *union with God* is somewhere in sight in all poetry, though it is usually rudimentary and misunderstood."[50] Lowell's early poetry reflects this "feeling," particularly in these lines from "A Prayer for my Grandfather to Our Lady" (*LWC* 28), the last section of "In Memory of Arthur Winslow":

> O Mother, I implore
> Your scorched, blue thunderbreasts of love to pour
> Buckets of blessings on my burning head
> Until I rise like Lazarus from the dead.

Our sophisticated sensibilities may balk at these lines, but Lowell is showing us something important here. As Bruce Michelson points out, "the central, grotesque metaphor . . . struggles to blend the mercy of the Virgin" with "the lost breast of the mother."[51] And in "Death from Cancer" (*LWC* 25), the first in this series of poems, Lowell imagines for his grandfather a vision of ultimate union, as Grandfather Winslow is carried "beyond Charles River to the Acheron / Where the wide waters and their voyager are one."

In the reminiscence that he wrote after Lowell's death, his friend Peter Taylor said that Lowell "was searching for a oneness in himself and a oneness in the world."[52] He conducted that search, as we know, through his poetry, and because of the nature of his mind and the circumstance of his illness, he used the methods of psychoanalysis as he searched. Such a search is never concluded, of course; Lowell knew that. But he lived his life, and he wrote his poetry, and much of the time he continued to believe that out there somewhere, "behind the next crook in the road or growth / of fog" there must be "a face, clock-white, still friendly to the earth" ("Harriet 1," *N* 21)—God, perhaps, or Lowell's wife, or a friend, maybe a therapist, or a lover—a face, an "other" through whom he might finally achieve that ultimate goal: "recognition of oneself as one knows oneself, and as one does not know oneself, but hopes to know."[53]

Lowell cannot always sustain his belief that there are meaningful others out there:

> Belief in God is an inclination to listen,
> but as we grow older and our freedom hardens,
> we hardly even want to hear ourselves . . .
> the silent universe our auditor—
> *I am to myself, and my trouble sings.*   [Lowell's ellipsis, *FLAH* 44]

But even as he describes his ultimate isolation, as he insists that *I am to myself*, he belies his own words. For his *trouble sings*. And as it sings it reaches out, as it does through all his poetry: in Lacan's words, "the function of language is not to inform but to evoke. What I seek in speech is the response of the other."[54]

> my house is empty. In our yard, the grass straggles. . . .
> I stand face to face with lost Love—my breath
> is life, the rough, the smooth, the bright, the drear.
>   [Lowell's ellipsis]

The title of this poem is "No Hearing."

4

A Poetry of Memory

"CHILDREN, the raging memory drools / Over the glory of past pools," Robert Lowell declaimed in his first volume of poetry ("The Drunken Fisherman," *LWC* 37). Throughout his career he would acknowledge again and again the power of memory in his poetry and in his life. By the time he wrote *Life Studies*, Lowell was using memory deliberately as a therapeutic instrument; many of the poems in that volume had their beginnings in prose reminiscences he wrote on the advice of his doctors. As we know, the use of memory to probe the past—to remember and to come to terms with conflicts that arise out of past experience—is one of the standard techniques of psychoanalysis and other forms of psychotherapy. According to Freud, "If a pathological idea . . . can be traced back to its elements in the patient's mental life from which it originated, it simultaneously crumbles away and the patient is freed from it."[1] Philip Rieff paraphrases Freud's definition of psychological illness as "the failure to become emancipated from one's past,"[2] and Rieff pinpoints the "peculiar and central place" of memory in psychoanalysis: "It is constraining, since by remembering our bondages to the past we appreciate their enormity; but it is also, Freud believed, liberating, since by remembering we understand the terrors and pleasures of the past and move toward mastering them."[3]

Jacques Lacan and others have stressed one particular aspect of this technique of using memory to investigate one's personal history. Concentrating on what Lacan calls the "intersubjective continuity of the discourse in which the subject's history is constituted," these psychoanalysts call for the subject to construct from his or her memories a personal narrative that will make sense of the past and its relation to the present.[4] But this approach too, as we shall see later in this chapter, has its detractors—critics who decry the emphasis on the continuity of the personal narrative. Here psychoanalysis confronts the problem of the nature of the self in the twentieth century. In his fine book *Being in the Text*, Paul Jay points to Henry Adams as the great enunciator not only of this problem but of a possible, if limited, solution. Both the problem and the solution are considered (and I use this next pun deliberately) in terms of language: "[Adams's] frank admission of the inadequacy of narrative as a form for modern self-representation and his conviction that the modern ego was a chaos of 'multiplicities' looks forward to a self-reflexive practice that articulates, and sometimes embraces, such a chaos."[5] This characterization of the self as a chaos of multiplicities to be embraced rather than as a tidy entity to be pinned down in a coherent narrative has its counterpart in contemporary theories of history. Given Lowell's lifelong habit of seeing himself as a reflection of history and history as a reflection of himself, we will need to consider at least briefly the application of these theories in Lowell's poetry.

We may appear to have wandered far from the subject of memory, but in fact memory, like association, like repetition, like relation, is inextricably bound up in our discussion of self-examination in Robert Lowell's poetry. His history was crucial in determining what he was to make of his self, both in his life and in his poetry, and he was well aware of the significance of memory in that process. Particularly in *For the Union Dead* and *Day by Day*, he addressed himself specifically to the question of the nature of that puzzling phenomenon. "Both fascinated and imprisoned by memories," John Crick says of the poet in *For the Union Dead*, "he seeks freedom through deliberate appropriations of them, and throughout the book weaves patterns of recollection."[6] The first four poems in the volume treat memory explicitly. In the first poem, "Water" (3), the poet addresses a woman with whom he has shared an experience in the past. "Remember?" he asks. "We sat on a slab of rock. / From this distance in time, / it seems the color / of iris, rotting and turning purpler." But the poet's memory errs: "it was only / the usual gray rock / turning the usual green / when drenched by the sea."

This knowledge of the distorting properties of memory hovers in the background throughout the rest of the volume, even when, as in the next poem, the poet expresses no doubts as to the accuracy of his recollections. The remembered past in "The Old Flame" (*FTUD* 5) is unpleasant: the poet and his wife were "quivering and fierce"; they lay "awake all night. / In one bed and apart," and listened to the snow-plow "groaning up hill." But now "Everything's changed for the best"—visiting the house in which the two had lived, the poet finds a "new landlord, / a new wife, a new broom." The house has been "swept bare, / furnished, garnished and aired," and the resulting sense of total discontinuity between past and present hints at what will become, for Lowell, one of the disturbing aspects of memory. Another of its alarming features takes concrete form in the next poem, "Middle Age" (*FTUD* 7). Lowell sets the scene, describing the "midwinter grind" of New York which "drills through [his] nerves" as he walks "the chewed-up streets." The dental imagery is unobtrusive enough to be effective and chilling, and thus to prepare the reader for the ominous next lines. "At forty-five, / what next, what next?" the poet asks. "At every corner, / I meet my Father, / my age, still alive." To come face to face with the father is terrifying, the more so since the poet at this stage of life has no answer to his own question. He has only the excruciating memory of the father in whose "dinosaur / death-steps" he must walk.

As is so often the case for Lowell, memory brings with it pain; he eschews autobiography in the next poem, "The Scream" (*FTUD* 8), which explores the way in which an uncomfortable memory acts upon a child. He bases the poem on "In the Village," a short story by Elizabeth Bishop about a young girl whose life is colored by the memory of her deranged mother's scream. Bishop begins her story with these words:

A scream, the echo of a scream, hangs over that Nova Scotian village. No one hears it; it hangs there forever, a slight stain in those pure blue skies . . . too dark, too blue, so that they seem to keep on darkening . . . over the woods and waters as well as the sky. The scream hangs like that, unheard, in memory—in the past, in the present, and those years between.[7]

The echo of a scream, hanging in memory, a slight stain in the sky, darkening over the woods and waters—this thinning echo becomes for Lowell a metaphor for memory itself.

In "The Scream," Lowell imagines memory as an echo thinning away, finally, to nothing, but much more often in *For the Union Dead* he insists upon its persistence. He plays with the notion of the instability of memory, the way remembered objects seem to change shape with the passage of time, as when, in "For the Union Dead" (*FTUD* 70), "The stone statues of the abstract Union Soldier / grow slimmer and younger each year." In that poem, as in "The Public Garden" (26) and "Returning" (34), the remembered past is superior to the present. Usually, however, the memories themselves are disappointing at best, and, at their worst, crippling. Lowell was taught that he must use his memory to explore the past in order better to understand the present, and in *For the Union Dead* he accepts the unpleasant truth that the darkening stain of memory colors the past with pain and grief. Later he will admit, "I return then, but not to what I wanted" ("Searchings 1," *N* 35).

Sometimes the memories cause pain because they reveal qualities in the young child that the remembering adult finds abhorrent. In "Florence" (*FTUD* 13), the poet remembers "How vulnerable the horseshoe crabs," which were "made for a child to grab / and throw strangling ashore!" Similarly, in "The Neo-Classical Urn" (*FTUD* 47), Lowell rubs his head and feels "a turtle shell," which he associates with memories of an early cruelty: he remembers "the plop and splash / of turtle on turtle" as he dropped the helpless creatures into a garden urn. In "Dunbarton," in *Life Studies* (65), the poet had recalled a similar incident from his childhood: catching and imprisoning newts in a tobacco tin, he saw himself "as a young newt, / neurasthenic, scarlet / and wild in the wild coffee-colored water"; in "The Neo-Classical Urn" he identifies himself not only with the turtles confined in the urn but also with their unfeeling captor: Lowell himself as a child. The garden urn is transmuted, in "Night Sweat" (*FTUD* 68), into the urn of the body, a container for memories:[8] "always inside me is the child who died."

Lowell's most extensive and thorough treatment of the subject of memory in *For the Union Dead* is "Eye and Tooth" (18), in which he dramatizes the complicated nature of that shadowy filter through which the poet sees the past. Irvin Ehrenpreis describes the poem in these words: "The poem depends on a brilliant use of the *eye-I* pun. Treating vision as memory or id, Lowell presents the voyeur poet's eye as an unwreckable showcase of displeasing memories that both shape and torment the person. The dominating metaphor is, so to speak, 'I've got something in my I and can't get it out.' "[9] This poem was not the first occasion on which Lowell had associated his eye and his I. Writing to Cousin Harriet in December of 1955, he describes "our first movie in two months, The eye of a Camera." But the typed words "The eye of" are crossed out, and written above them in Elizabeth Hardwick's handwriting are the words "I am"; at the end of the letter she has added a note saying that "You will see the marks of my editing here."[10] And in "Near the Unbalanced Aquarium," one of the prose reminiscences that Lowell wrote as part of his therapy, and which would serve as the basis for some of the poems in *Life Studies*, he made this association explicit. "Nearly blind with myopia" as a result of having dropped his eyeglasses from a third-story window, "I was reborn each time I saw my blurred, now unspectacled, now unprofessorial face in the mirror."[11] Here the fuzzy vision has the potential to banish bad memories, to give him a fresh start; but as the rest of the story makes clear, no such beginning is forthcoming.

"Eye and Tooth," too, begins with a juxtaposition of the eye and the I:

My whole eye was sunset red,
the old cut cornea throbbed,
I saw things darkly,
as through an unwashed goldfish globe.

As the rest of the poem will make clear, the "old cut cornea" represents among other things, in Stephen Yenser's words, "the flaw in man's nature, original sin, which 'Nothing can dislodge.' "[12] "My eyes throb," the poet complains in the fourth stanza. "Nothing can dislodge / the house with my first tooth / noosed in a knot to the doorknob." Apparently remembering an incident from his childhood, Lowell here represents this memory of an unpleasant experience as a tangible, physical object in his eye (I).

The association of memory with sin begins in the next stanzas, which, as several critics have noticed, are closely related to a prose passage in Lowell's essay on William Carlos Williams:

> An image held my mind . . .—an old-fashioned New England cottage freshly painted white. I saw a shaggy, triangular shade on the house, trees, a hedge, or their shadows, the blotch of decay. The house . . . came from the time when I was a child, still unable to read, and living in the small town of Barnstable on Cape Cod. Inside the house was a bird book with an old stiff and steely engraving of a sharp-shinned hawk. The hawk's legs had a reddish-brown buffalo fuzz on them; behind was the blue sky, bare and abstracted from the world.[13]

In his description of the triangular shade on the house, the shadows, "the blotch of decay," we may perhaps sense a similarity to the darkening stain of memory Lowell adapted from Elizabeth Bishop in "The Scream." In any event, the poet in "Eye and Tooth" juxtaposes the memory of the triangular blotch with the remembered image of the hawk, whose cold eye seemed to pronounce judgment on the small boy:

> Nothing can dislodge
> the triangular blotch
> of rot on the red roof,
> a cedar hedge, or the shade of a hedge.

> No ease from the eye
> of the sharp-shinned hawk in the birdbook there,
> with reddish brown buffalo hair
> on its shanks, one ascetic talon

> clasping the abstract imperial sky.
> It says:
> *an eye for an eye,*
> *a tooth for a tooth.*

The eye is both judge and instrument of punishment, the super-ego made concrete. And the eye is the instrument of the crime as well:

No ease for the boy at the keyhole,
his telescope,
when the women's white bodies flashed
in the bathroom. Young, my eyes began to fail.

As Alan Holder has pointed out, we learn in "Art of the Possible"
(*DBD* 36) that "for a winter or so, / when eleven or twelve," the
poet "nightly enjoyed [his] mother bathing" in the bathroom; and
there is no ease for the boy, no ease from the eye, no ease, now,
for the man whose eyes are full of memories.[14]

Nothing! No oil
for the eye, nothing to pour
on those waters or flames.
I am tired. Everyone's tired of my turmoil.

To surrender to memories can be exhausting, draining, both for
the poet and for his readers. Richard Fein explores this aspect of
memory when he discusses "Eye and Tooth" and several other
poems in *For the Union Dead*:

These poems show us that the poem that springs from a pain-
ful memory does not necessarily offer the poet a release. In-
deed, the overwrought memory can be a stumbling block in
the way of recovery from the past. Memory can be freedom,
but it can also be oppression. If remembering the past allows
a person to understand and assuage that past, it is also true
that one can become fascinated and obsessed with such mem-
ories, which then undercut his ability to release himself from
the past.[15]

After *For the Union Dead*, Lowell continued to address the question
of the puzzling nature of memory, and in several poems he came
to conclusions that reinforce Fein's pessimistic view of its power. "I
pray for memory," he begins a late poem, and remembering, iden-
tifies himself with the "Turtle" (*DBD* 98).

I pray for memory—
an old turtle,
absentminded, inelastic,

kept afloat by losing touch . . .
no longer able to hiss or lift
a useless shield against the killer.   [Lowell's ellipsis]

The turtle is helpless but brave, and Lowell, emphasizing the false
sense of security a turtle or a poet feels inside his shell, describes
him as naive but courageous and admirable: "Turtles age, but
wade out amorously, / half-frozen fossils, yet knight-errant / in a
foolsdream of armor." In "Long Summer 4" (*N* 25), Lowell had
used the figure of a turtle to underline his sense of human vulner-
ability enclosed within a shell of seeming imperviousness:

> . . . I flame for the one friend—
> is it always the same child or animal
> impregnable in shell or coat of thorns,
> only kept standing by a hundred scared habits—
> turtle the deft hand tips on its back with a stick?

The feeling of helplessness implicit in this passage is raised to
another power at the end of "Turtle." His memory triggered by the
sight of three snapping turtles in his bedroom, Lowell remembers
the turtles he caught as a child, and, acknowledging "the rawness
that let us meet as animals," imagines a horrible, compensatory
scenario:

> . . . Too many pictures
> have screamed from the reel . . . in the rerun,
> the snapper holds on till sunset—
> in the awful instantness of retrospect,
> its beak
> works me underwater drowning by my neck,
> as it claws away pieces of my flesh
> to make me small enough to swallow.   [Lowell's ellipsis]

Memory itself has become the old turtle that the poet prayed for at
the beginning of the poem—a creature often attractive and appeal-
ing, but liable, "in the awful instantness of retrospect," to swallow
us alive.

In "Grass Fires" (*DBD* 85), Lowell approaches the subject of
memory differently, beginning in a discursive, matter-of-fact tone:

> In the realistic memory
> the memorable must be forgone;
> it never matters,
> except in front of our eyes.

Or, as Mark Rudman suggests: "out of sight, out of mind."[16] But perhaps it is not so simple; isn't "the memorable" often "in front of our eyes" whether we want it there or not? In fact, isn't that precisely the problem?

> I made it a warning,
> a cure, that stabilized nothing.
> We cannot recast the faulty drama,
> play the child,
> unable to align
> his toppling, elephantine script,
> the hieroglyphic letters
> he sent home.

Even memory used specifically as a cure-all is ineffective: what happened, happened. But, again, isn't the meaning of this passage undercut like the meaning of the first four lines? Isn't Lowell always playing the child, writing his hieroglyphic letters? And doesn't he recognize that fact, and play with it here?

And now, the memory itself:

> I hold big kitchen matches to flaps of frozen grass
> to smoke a rabbit from its hole—
> then the wind bites them, then they catch,
> the grass catches, fire everywhere,
> everywhere
> inextinguishable roots,
> the tree grandfather planted for his shade,
> combusting, towering
> over the house he anachronized with stone.

Here Rudman discusses Lowell's "belief that if you touched the point of pain it spread everywhere and that everyone was graced and afflicted with 'inextinguishable roots,' something most people would like to forget—not their origins but that nothing could be undone."[17] But can the past be "undone," can the fire be put out, are our roots indeed inextinguishable? Lowell keeps us in suspense for a few lines, then ends the poem:

> The fire-engines deployed with stage bravado,
> yet it was I put out the fire,
> who slapped it to death with my scarred leather jacket.
> I snuffed out the inextinguishable root,
> I—
> really I can do little,
> as little now as then,
> about the infernal fires—
> I cannot blow out a match.

There is a terrible poignancy in that isolated, suspended "I," because it begins as self-confident self-assertion, emphatic repetition of the fact of decisive action, but even as it is being uttered it is changing to a confession of complete inadequacy. And since the small boy whose experience is being remembered here in fact did act, did put out the fire, the feeling of inadequacy is doubly distressing. The memory here, which would seem to bolster the rememberer's sense of self-worth, instead draws him into a state close to despair.

Laurence Lieberman, discussing "Turtle" and other poems in *Day by Day*, concludes that in some of these poems Lowell finds memory simply too difficult and too dangerous. In "Shifting Colors" (119), for example, Lieberman points to the lines "I am too weak to strain to remember, or give / recollection the eye of a microscope" and he has this to say about the poem as a whole: "Lowell had grown to regard the exercise of his retrospective faculty as being hazardous to his physical well-being, often dragging him down to a pit of hopeless enervation. And in pursuit of a new self-protective creed, a healing balm, he found he must abandon his powers of memory altogether."[18] Certainly *Day by Day* contains poems in which memory acts cruelly—"Home" (113) and "Unwanted" (121), for example, are almost unbearable to read— but it is also true that many of the poems in the volume reflect a gentler memory, a memory that heals; as is true throughout his career, Lowell in his last volume is ambivalent about memory and its powers and uses.

In "Unwanted," the poem in which Lowell confronts his knowledge that he was "an unwanted child," he writes these lines:

causes for my misadventure, considered
for forty years too obvious to name,
come jumbling out
to give my simple autobiography a plot.

In Lowell's eagerness to give his "simple autobiography" a plot, we encounter not only an aesthetic desire but also a primary focus of some schools of psychoanalysis and psychotherapy. At the beginning of this chapter we mentioned Jacques Lacan's reference to "the intersubjective continuity of the discourse in which the subject's history is constituted"; this "intersubjective continuity" might be otherwise described as the "plot" that gives coherence to the "story" of one's life. Autobiography is the traditional genre in which we see this story worked out on the page, and Roy Pascal confirms the therapeutic nature of that elusive genre when he describes it as "an interplay, a collusion, between past and present; its significance is indeed more the revelation of the present situation than the uncovering of the past."[19] The agent of this uncovering of the past is, obviously, memory, and James Olney describes its function: "It is through the operation of memory, which draws all the significant past up into the focus of the present, that the autobiographer and the poet succeed in universalizing their experience and their meaning. Each of them discovers, in fact, by looking through the glass of memory, a meaning in his experience which was not there before and which exists now only as a present creation."[20]

By referring to his *Selected Poems* as "autobiography . . . a small-scale *Prelude*," Lowell made it inevitable that his readers would consider the similarities between Wordsworth's monumental project and Lowell's own—and *Selected Poems* is monumental because it is, after all, only a synecdoche for the entire vast body of Lowell's poetry.[21] But Lowell cautioned that his poems do not tell a story of "the growth of a poet's mind," and we may conclude by the end of this chapter that Wordsworth and Lowell use memory in ways that are in fact profoundly different. But the two share at least a predilection for exploring their individual pasts with the hope of better understanding the present, and in the course of their explorations of the past both poets revert again and again to the metaphor of the journey. In his discussion of Wordsworth's poetry, Richard Onorato says that "the journey metaphor suggests . . . that one goes toward the eternal and the infinite, as for instance in the Christian pilgrimage of life, through death to eternal life. But there is also very strongly the suggestion of 'returning' in that journey 'home' to the place one left, or of returning to the condition that obtained before the search or journey began."[22]

This metaphor of the journey "home" has profound metaphysical as well as psychological implications, and Lowell not only returned "home" through memory in his poems, but he ruminated on the nature of those returns as well. In the title poem in *For the Union Dead* (70), he returns to the "old South Boston Aquarium" and admits, in a haunting phrase, that "I often sigh still / for the dark downward and vegetating kingdom / of the fish and reptile." He treats the theme explicitly in the same volume in the poem "Returning" (34), which he says in a Note (1) was suggested by Giuseppi Ungaretti's "Canzone." Stephen Yenser has pointed out that the poet here is "returning" after the "dark night" of the preceding poem, "Myopia: a Night."[23] Here the poet is ambivalent about his return. He brags that "the dogs still know me by my smell," but all the same, it's "rather a dead town / after my twenty year's mirage." The poet is in a state of enervation like that of a person recovering from an episode of mania:

> Long awash,
> breaking myself against the surf,
> touching bottom, rushed
> by the green go-light
> of those nervous waters, I found
> my exhaustion, the light of the world.

"Nothing is deader than this small town main street," he continues. The "venerable elm sickens" and "no leaf / is born."

Helen Vendler tells us that Ungaretti "describes in his 'Canzone' an immobile Hades where no leaf is born or falls, nothing wakes or slumbers, and there is neither light nor shadow, nor past nor future. This is, says Ungaretti, 'the crossing over, with sensual experience exhausted, of the threshold of another experience . . . the Pascalian knowing of being out of the null. Horrid consciousness. Its odyssey always has as its point of departure the past, always returns to conclude itself in the past.' "[24] Lowell, too, returns to conclude in the past.

> But I remember its former fertility,
> how everything came out clearly
> in the hour of credulity
> and young summer, when this street
> was already somewhat overshaded,
> and here at the altar of surrender,
> I met you,
> the death of thirst in my brief flesh.

The poet, having returned at the beginning of the poem to a place, a "sheltered little resort" that he finds changed, now returns in memory to an earlier, happier time. The "you" whom he meets is undeniably a girl—"All life's grandeur / is something with a girl in summer" he will say later ("Waking Early Sunday Morning," *NTO* 13). But, as Yenser convincingly argues, Lowell may refer also to Christ (or, as I prefer, to Mary); in either case the reference is to Lowell's conversion to Catholicism.[25] The next lines sustain this interpretation. "That was the first growth," Lowell says; "more and more it grew green, and gave too much shelter." But the possessive smothering of girl or church is part of the past; "now at my homecoming, / . . . / I am a foot taller than when I left."

The poet ends with a feeling of malaise:

> Yet sometimes I catch my vague mind
> circling with a glazed eye
> for a name without a face, or a face without a name,
> and at every step,
> I startle them. They start up,
> dog-eared, bald as baby birds.

The words, "bald as baby birds," refer back to the "bald-headed" members of the poet's old "gang" with whom he began the poem: figures from the past who keep popping up in his memory. And the vague mind, "circling" without rest "for a name without a face, or a face without a name"—what is it searching for? Perhaps the speaker is simply looking for a woman, any anonymous woman. Or perhaps here is confirmation of Yenser's suggestion that the poet is remembering his brief immersion in the comfortable security of belief in God; the poet sounds here like the loving father in "Harriet 1" (*N* 21), who, detailing the child's successive attempts to characterize God, ends in an automobile, headlights probing the fog, searching for "a face, clock-white, still friendly to the earth."

Lowell rewrote "Returning" for *Day by Day*, transposing it into the leaner, more fluid "Homecoming" (11). He begins the poem with the statement "What was is"; because there is no comma between the two verbs, the reader is free to turn the statement into an ironic question designed to demonstrate the fact that in the moment of reading (or writing), the past is already changing to the present. But we know that this poem is a revision of "Returning," so we interpret the words instead to mean that the poet has come "home" to a place that has remained unchanged. This interpretation in its turn must be revised, because Lowell immediately undercuts his assertion by giving an example of radical change: "the boys in my old gang / are senior partners." So the reader tries again: she assumes (with an implied comma between the verbs) that "what was is" not in the reality of the homecoming (which is no reality, of course, but rather the reality of the poem in which we choose to believe), but in the poet's memory. But in fact his memories have also changed since the time of the writing of "Returning." The "you" whom he meets "in the hour of credulity" is purely secular here; there is no suggestion of God or Catholicism, but rather a girl who shares "the nights we made it / on our *Vesuvio* martinis / with no vermouth but vodka / to sweeten the dry gin." Despite the first line, the poet here, as in "Returning," senses a change, a decline in fertility and health. He uses clean, sparse lines to emphasize his point: "things gone wrong / clothe summer / with gold leaf." In this dry time he searches for what he no longer has:

Sometimes
I catch my mind
circling for you with glazed eye—
my lost love hunting
your lost face.

He has come home, but he cannot find what he is seeking, cannot reclaim the past: "it's a town for the young, / they break themselves against the surf. / No dog knows my smell."

In this poem, Lowell's attitude toward homecoming is not ambivalent but decisively negative. One can go home again but to no avail: he remembers and learns nothing useful, nothing that can help him understand his present. Nevertheless, it is necessary to return, to come back, to go home—as he informs us in "Pigeons" (*I* 149). Although Lowell arranged his *Imitations* in chronological order from Homer through Pasternak, he placed Rilke's "Pigeons" at the end of the volume, apart from the other Rilke poems; perhaps emphasizing by its position the poet's intention to return from his voyage into the poetic territory of others and to come home to his own individual work. He begins with this passage:

> The same old flights, the same old homecomings,
> dozens of each per day,
> but at last the pigeon gets clear of the pigeon-house . . .
> What is home, but a feeling of homesickness
> for the flight's lost moment of fluttering terror? [Lowell's ellipsis]

The reader feels trapped in the first two lines, unable to break out of the rigid three-stress meter, unable to break out of the unending cycle of flights and returns. Here homecoming is not a willed act, not a deliberate return through memory to the time and place of one's origin, but rather a compulsive gesture. "Home" is no refuge here, no source of strength, but rather a stifling, closed-in situation or condition; then, when "at last the pigeon gets clear of the pigeon-house," the dactyls speed us along into flights of freedom. As the next line makes clear, even a "moment of fluttering terror" is better than the constraints of "home." Throughout the poem, home retains its connotations of limitation and suppression, while flight means liberation and energy. Nevertheless, the pigeon and the person always return.

> Over non-existence arches the all-being—
> thence the ball thrown almost out of bounds
> stings the hand with the momentum of its drop—
> body and gravity,
> miraculously multiplied by its mania to return.

Yenser suggests that Lowell used "imaginative license" in translating these lines, and points out that the last words, "mania to return," echo the imaginatively rendered "mania of Achilles" in the first line of the first poem in the volume (Homer's "The Killing of Lykaon"). Clearly, he says, "Lowell intends 'to return' us to the volume's initial line."[26] But we sense in this poem no therapeutic benefit in a return through memory to one's home, but rather compulsive cycles of flight and return that resemble the stifling repetition compulsion discussed in chapter 2.

In addition to these poems, Lowell wrote a matched pair of poems, strategically placed in his career, which consider obliquely the question of a return through memory to one's origins: "The Exile's Return," the first poem in *Lord Weary's Castle* (9), and "Ulysses and Circe," the first poem in *Day by Day* (3). "The Exile's Return" was written in 1946, before there is any reason to suppose that Lowell had any but the most general kind of knowledge about psychoanalysis; he certainly did not intend in any conscious way that his exile should represent a man returning through memory to his past. But in light of what he does with this same theme in "Ulysses and Circe," which Ian Hamilton calls a "rewriting" of "The Exile's Return," we are justified in noticing how neatly the poem fits into the category of homecoming poems we have been discussing.[27]

Richard Onorato, speaking of the journey metaphor, observes that the "epic sense of journey, derived by Wordsworth from Milton, has its most precise analogue in *The Odyssey*."[28] And Robert Lowell, profoundly influenced by Milton, was especially interested in Ulysses. "The Exile's Return," according to Hugh Staples, "is the theme of the Odyssey with an unhappy ending: here the return is not to Ithaca but to a Land of Unlikeness."[29] Elaborating on Staples's discovery that Lowell has put into his poem "nearly all of the imagery and even the exact phraseology of the opening pages of [Thomas Mann's] *Tonio Kröger*," Philip Cooper has this to say: " 'The Exile's Return' fables again the disappointment, dispossession, disinheritance a man finds when he tries to recover the lost promises of childhood. Tonio Kröger . . . tries to go home again as a grown man and finds himself mistaken for a criminal."[30] It is not surprising that Robert Lowell, at the time of writing this poem, should feel kinship to Tonio Kröger, who was mistaken for a criminal; Lowell himself had just been released from prison, where he had served time as a conscientious objector during World War II. He had come "home," and his feelings were ambivalent. As he was to do so often throughout his career, Lowell in this poem incorporates his own history into that of the world at large: the returning prisoner is the returning American soldier is the returning German exile. And all of these in turn are the poet, though this particular patrician poet would never make explicit such a Whitmanesque identity.

The exile returns, in Staples's words, to a "Land of Unlikeness." Nothing is as it was, the war has changed everything, and the country is harsh and unwelcoming:

> . . . A bell
> Grumbles when the reverberations strip
> The thatching from its spire,
> The search-guns click and spit and split up timber
> And nick the slate roofs on the Holstenwall
> Where torn-up tilestones crown the victor. . . .

The reader reading these lines enacts the experience of the exile who expects a smooth welcome home and instead is obstructed at every turn. What Harvey Gross, speaking of another Lowell poem, calls "a splutter of consonants" here causes the reader to pause after the many words that end in "k" or "p" or "t" sounds. The meter, too, obstructs the reader. Gross has said that the "striking feature of the metric of *Lord Weary's Castle* is its overwhelming physicality. Lines clang and grind; the movement stops dead and resumes with a shudder; stress jams against stress until lines break under the tension."[31] In these lines the movement stops dead after "grumbles"; stress jams against stress in "The search-guns click and spit and split up timber / And nick the slate roofs on the Holstenwall." By the time the reader reaches the "gray, sorry and ancestral house / Where the dynamited walnut tree / Shadows a squat, old, wind-torn gate" (stress jamming against stress again), she is exhausted. But there is some cause for hope:

> . . . already lily-stands
> Burgeon the risen Rhineland, and a rough

Cathedral lifts its eye. Pleasant enough,
Voi ch'entrate, and your life is in your hands.

The words flow more smoothly here, and the Lowell of 1946
would have considered the cathedral a welcome and welcoming
sight. Staples considers the ending a "calm, understated promise
of renascence" until undercut by "the ominous Dantean overtones
of the last line."[32] *Voi ch'entrate*, he tells us, "is, of course, part of
the inscription over the Gate of Hell, as described by Dante in
Inferno, III, 9. The full phrase is . . . 'Abandon all hope, ye who
enter.' "[33] For Randall Jarrell this is an "unhappy ending"; the
"menacing *Voi ch'entrate* . . . transforms the exile's old home into a
place where even hope must be abandoned."[34] But I am not con-
vinced. For a reader who knows that Lowell has thirty years after
the date of this poem in which to write poetry, and that the subject
of his poetry was so often to be the person of Robert Lowell him-
self, the last words offer some hope. "Your life is in your hands,"
he tells the exile who has returned to his "gray, sorry and ances-
tral house"—the exile who is, of course, among others, himself.
The place that the exile comes home to may be "pleasant enough"
or it may be hell. The poet will make his own life by writing about
it, and much of what he writes will be the product of memories of
his own ancestral house.

On his return to the United States from England in the fall of
1973, Lowell "wrote nine poems in a relaxed, almost meandering
free verse. . . . They were . . . about returning from exile (indeed,
one of them was a rewriting of a poem from *Lord Weary's Castle*
called 'Exile's Return'); the poet sees himself as Ulysses 'circling'
the geography of the life he left behind."[35] The poem that would
become "Ulysses and Circe" was to be included, eventually, in
Day by Day (3); this last volume of Lowell's poetry, which Helen
Vendler reviewed under the heading "The Poetry of Autobiogra-
phy," was in itself a kind of return, a recapitulation of lifelong
concerns.[36] In "Ulysses and Circe," which in an early version was
entitled "Ulysses, Circe, Penelope," the situation of the poet-voy-
ager after his return to Ithaca constitutes a substantial part of the
poem. In the next-to-last section, immediately before the return,
Lowell has Ulysses address Circe in words that look back to the
earlier "Returning":

"Long awash and often touching bottom
by the sea's great green go-light
I found my exhaustion
the light of the world.["]

From Lowell's drafts, it is clear that he began the poem in a personal rather than a mythic mode; Circe is clearly Caroline and Penelope, Elizabeth.[37] One draft is entitled "Homecoming," and in several drafts, one entitled "Nantucket," he speaks in the first person:

No one saw my flight and voyage back
rounding Nantucket's green and white,
if this could ever happen—
on foot and visible,
my walk from the dock to my house.
It was remarked on,
my eyes were on my toes.
You preceded me, my figurehead,
the blowing, sacklike black shift
you wore when pregnant.

In the final version, this section of the poem is entitled "Penelope" and we watch the same scene as though from a distance:

She sees no feat
in his flight or his flight back—
ten years to and ten years fro.
On foot and visible,
he walks from Long Wharf home.
Nobody in Ithaca knows him,
and yet he is too much remarked.

Walking "from Long Wharf home," he remembers the past, "twenty years ago, / . . . when he enticed Penelope / to dance herself to coma in his arms," and contrasts it with the present:

. . . Today his house
is more convivial and condescending;
she is at home,

well furnished with her entourage,
her son, her son's friends, her lovers—

He "enters the house," but "mistakes / a daughter for her mother."
"It is not surprising," we are told. Ulysses is allowed inside his
home for the space of eight lines, then ejected by the suitors.

He is outdoors;
his uninvited hands are raw, they say
I love you through the locked window.
At forty, she is still
the best bosom in the room.
He looks at her,
she looks at him admiring her,
then turns to the suitors . . .

Like the young boy at the keyhole in "Eye and Tooth," Ulysses is
reduced to the status of observer, peering at women's bodies
from an outside vantage point. But he is not helpless: "he circles
as a shark circles / visibly behind the window," waiting, as Helen
Vendler tells us, for the moment when he will murder the suit-
ors,[38] and perhaps Penelope as well. The poet-traveler has gone
"ten years fro and ten years to," and to what purpose? There is
nothing left at home for him—no solace, no self-knowledge. He is
left in limbo, circling, alone. And as a line in one of the drafts
reveals, "not a wink or a shiver betrays the pain of the shark."

Lowell uses myth in "Ulysses and Circe" to distance himself
from the hard fact of his discovery (at least for the duration of this
poem) that he cannot invent a narrative that will satisfactorily con-
nect the past with the present. And throughout his career he used
not only myth but other structures—religion, psychoanalysis, his-
tory—in an attempt to fit his own experience into some sort of
coherent pattern. Alan Williamson points to one such pattern
when he says that, beginning with *Near the Ocean* and *Notebook*, "it
becomes reasonable to speak of Lowell's 'system,' as one would of
Yeats's; for the personal-public analogy *is* the overriding structure
of the poem."[39] And, indeed, from time to time throughout his
career, Lowell identifies his own childhood, as it exists in his
memory, with the beginning of humankind. Sometimes he stresses
the sinister aspects of Eden, as in "Christmas Eve Under Hooker's

Statue" (*LWC* 23): "Twenty years ago / I hung my stocking on the tree, and hell's / Serpent entwined the apple in the toe / To sting the child with knowledge." Sometimes he revels in the memory of a more pleasant Eden; in "The Public Garden" (*FTUD* 26), he puts into the speaker's mouth (with minor changes) lines he originally gave to Anne Kavanaugh in "The Mills of the Kavanaughs":

Remember summer? Bubbles filled
the fountain, and we splashed. We drowned
in Eden, while Jehovah's grass-green lyre
was rustling all about us in the leaves
that gurgled by us, turning upside down. . . . [Lowell's ellipsis]

And sometimes he merges his own childhood into classical history. In the "Mother and Son" poem in "Between the Porch and the Altar" (*LWC* 47), the poet as an adult confronts his mother, who makes him "lose ten years, / Or is it twenty?"

. . . the son retires
Into the sack and selfhood of the boy
Who clawed through fallen houses of his Troy,
Homely and human only when the flames
Crackle in recollection. . . .

Although the theory is now discredited, the idea of a relationship between the childhood of an individual and the early periods of human history was developed early in the history of psychoanalysis. Larry David Nachman's discussion of Freudian theory and method in "Psychoanalysis and Social Theory" gives a concise account of Karl Abraham's theory, later adopted by Freud; Abraham, Nachman says, "turned to the embryological discovery that ontogeny recapitulates phylogeny, that the developing embryo passes through the varying stages of evolution. He asserted that in the same way the psychological development of the individual recapitulated the stages of human history. The earliest period of human history corresponded to the early stages of childhood."[40] Lowell turns this theory into poetry in *History*; in this volume, the history of the world and the history of Robert Lowell are inseparable. In "Our Fathers" (26), after identifying the "tyrannosaur" with "the neanderthal, first anthropoid to laugh," Lowell has this to say about humankind and himself:

> we lack staying power, though we will to live.
> Abel learned this falling among the jellied
> creepers and morning-glories of the saurian sunset.
> But was there some shining, grasping hand to guide
> me when I breathed through gills, and walked on fins
> through Eden . . . ?

Lowell makes no distinction between his individual past and that of humankind, between what he remembers of his childhood and what we know of the "saurian sunset," the dawn of history. In "In Genesis" (26), the poem that immediately precedes "Our Fathers" in *History*, Lowell shows how closely he must have been reading Freud's speculations about what he "would come to call the 'archaic heritage,' the notion that Freud stubbornly maintained . . . that there existed biologically inherited memories."[41] Unlike Jung's notion of the collective unconscious, Freud's "archaic heritage" was grounded in biology rather than myth and religion. From the time of "Totem and Taboo" through "Moses and Monotheism" Freud developed his theory: "what may be operative in an individual's psychical life may include not only what he has experienced himself but also things that were innately present in him at his birth, elements with a phylogenetic origin. . . . the archaic heritage of human beings comprises not only dispositions but also subject-matter—memory traces of the experience of earlier generations."[42] To account for the origin of guilt, Freud posited a primal crime that each person throughout history "remembers": "One day the brothers who had been driven out came together, killed and devoured their father."[43] With this rather understated account by Freud, compare Lowell's version:

> . . . Orpheus in Genesis
> hacked words from brute sound, and taught men English,
> plucked all the flowers, deflowered all the girls
> with the overemphasis of a father.

He used too many words, his sons killed him,
dancing with grateful gaiety round the cookout.

["In Genesis," H 26]

This poem, which should fan the fears of "strong" poets who fear competition from those who come after them, demonstrates the lighter side of Lowell's fascination with history and with his place in it—with his story. But in *The Psychoanalytic Dialogue*, Stanley Leavy devotes considerable attention to the serious relationship between psychoanalysis and history, the ways in which psychoanalysis "makes history." Leavy argues that "it is impossible to exaggerate the importance of the ideas of history and prehistory for psychoanalysis. That which has been lived in the person's past is the substance of both preconscious memory— the past that can be made present at will—and of unconscious memory—the past that can be inferred and constructed out of preconscious elements. Such an identity—the lived past with its historical-psychoanalytic recall—is a presupposition of our work." There is, of course, a great difference "between personal history and the history of societies": "In psychoanalysis all is 'subjective' . . . What counts is the uniquely private slant on the events being narrated, and what counts least is whether or not anyone else's view of them would concur."[44]

But it is precisely this "uniquely private slant," with its concomitant assumption that the individual can form a coherent narrative of history—whether private or public—which is in question in Lowell's poetry. Michel Foucault, in "Nietzsche, Genealogy, History," offers a careful analysis of Nietzsche's concept of "effective" history:

"Effective" history differs from traditional history in being without constants. Nothing in man—not even his body—is sufficiently stable to serve as the basis for self-recognition or for understanding other men. The traditional devices for constructing a comprehensive view of history and for retracing the past as a patient and continuous development must be systematically dismantled. . . . Knowledge, even under the banner of history, does not depend on "rediscovery," and it emphatically excludes the "rediscovery of ourselves." History

becomes "effective" to the degree that it introduces disconti-
nuity into our very being.[45]

Foucault helpfully ties together the private and the public aspects
of history here and thus makes it easy for us to see the relevance
of Nietzsche's theories to psychoanalysis. Roy Schafer, in *Narrative
Actions in Psychoanalysis*, objects specifically to the "implausible
tidiness" of the "simplified linear narratives" that are likely to
emerge from psychoanalysis, and suggests rather that the narra-
tions should "convey in some form the drama of the quest, with
all its uncertainties and difficulties, and the timelessness of the
mode of investigation itself."[46]

When Shafer suggests that "the timelessness of the mode of
investigation itself" is a subject for consideration in the untidy
narration that would be his ideal, he reminds us that we are, after
all, dealing here with a poet, Robert Lowell, who throughout his
life was conscientiously writing his own version of his own his-
tory, and writing about writing that history. In *Being in the Text*,
the pun in the title becomes crucial as Paul Jay traces the implica-
tions of autobiographical writers from Augustine through Roland
Barthes, and finds a gradual evolution into what he calls a "discur-
sive mode":

> A *discursive* mode . . . which fully situates the writer's self in
> the moments of its composition in his text, seeks to avoid
> the ontological contradiction in autobiographical narration be-
> tween the writer and his subject, while it also represents the
> abandonment of the kind of therapeutic hope . . . in Augus-
> tine, Wordsworth, and Proust. Whether such a discursive
> mode . . . can be more truthful about the self than a narrative
> mode is another matter.[47]

As we have seen at the beginning of this chapter, Jay uses
Henry Adams as an example of one who understood the inade-
quacy of narrative as a form for modern self-representation. As
James E. B. Breslin and Robert Giroux have pointed out,[48] Lowell
began "Antebellum Boston," one of his prose reminiscences, with
a deliberate echo of the beginning of *The Education of Henry Adams*:
"I, too, was born under the shadow of the Boston State House,

and under Pisces, the Fish, on the first of March 1917. America was entering the First World War. . . . Nothing from now on was to go quite as expected—even downhill."[49] Lowell apparently wrote "Antebellum Boston" around the same time as the other reminiscences that became the basis for *Life Studies*, and it seems clear from that volume that the effort to make a coherent narrative out of his memories seemed sometimes too difficult—or perhaps too easy. In a letter to Alan Williamson, the poet said that he had "read ⅔ of Freud, like reading Tolstoy. In that sense (memory, randomly renewed), Life Studies is full of him."[50] Lowell's sense that the volume depends on "memory, randomly renewed" corresponds to the views of many readers; Lawrence Kramer, for example, calls the poems "isolated segments of an unrealized narrative" and suggests that the poetry "does not act out a process of recollection but unfolds instead as an inventory of recollections."[51] A. Kingsley Weatherhead describes the volume as "a series of individual anecdotal stories that individually lack narrative coherence and together do not make up a life."[52] Karl Malkoff suggests that in this volume "Lowell fragments experience into a series of intersecting planes rather than a sequential narrative,"[53] and James E. B. Breslin details the steps Lowell took in abandoning the more coherent "prose project" that he had undertaken at the behest of his psychiatrists in favor of the "more discontinuous representation of his life that we get in the 'Life Studies' sequence."[54]

In "Near the Unbalanced Aquarium," part of that "prose project" to which Breslin refers, Lowell articulates a concept that may help us to understand the nature of his attitude toward the efficacy of narrative—as it applies to his efforts to understand himself as well as to write poetry: "One morning in July 1954 I sat in my bedroom on the third floor of the Payne-Whitney clinic of New York Hospital, trying as usual to get my picture of myself straight. I was recovering from a violent manic seizure, an attack of pathological enthusiasm. . . . My mind, somewhat literary and somewhat musclebound, hunted for the clue to the right picture of itself."[55] "The right picture of itself"—the snapshot, the image pinned down in a static form so that it can be studied and perhaps understood, even if only for a moment—this "picture" becomes for Lowell an alternative to story, to narrative. "I hoped in *Life Studies*," Lowell said, although "it was a limitation—that each poem might seem as open and single-surfaced as a photograph."[56]

These quick sketches, "life studies," tell a truth that the poet keeps coming back to throughout his life and his poetry.

In a review essay on *Day by Day*, J. D. McClatchy notes that "the most recurrent image in the book—the photograph—takes on an emblematic quality. Snapshots, actual or figurative, as spots of time to be revisited, recalculated, revalued."[57] Besides reminding us once again of Wordsworth's use of memory in his poetry, McClatchy's comment encourages us to see *Day by Day* as the resolution—though a final resolution only because death cut off the life and the poetry—of a conflict that had been present in Lowell's poetry of self-examination since its beginning. The urge to fit the life and the poetry into an order, a form—either a "preexisting" order like religion or myth or history, or a narrative order of his own construction—competed throughout his life with the countervailing impulse to embrace the fragmentary, the momentary, and to find in them what would suffice.[58] In both these endeavors he used memory, and in *Day by Day*, that quintessential volume of returnings through memory to the past, Lowell finally seems able to encompass both modes rather than struggling to decide on one or the other.

In the snapshot poems of *Day by Day*, the poet seems to be committing himself to the primacy of the glimpse, the moment in which the "musclebound" mind of the poet can find "the right picture of itself." But the reality is not so simple; the "50 years of snapshots" he praises in "Our Afterlife I" (21) are themselves part of "an account / accumulating layer and angle, / face and profile." And "Epilogue" (127), the justly famous last poem in *Day by Day* (not counting an appendix of translations, which raises interesting questions relevant to our discussion in chapter 3 of Lowell's poetry as a poetry of relation), embodies these same kinds of contradictions.

> Those blessèd structures, plot and rhyme—
> why are they no help to me now
> I want to make
> something imagined, not recalled?

He has aspired to the "painter's vision," which "trembles to caress the light." But his own work seems only

> . . . a snapshot,
> lurid, rapid, garish, grouped,
> heightened from life,
> yet paralyzed by fact.
> All's misalliance.

Several drafts of this poem bear the title "Facts."[59] The implication of this title is that, for Lowell, the "snapshots" seemed to him "only" "facts"—miscellaneous, various, and therefore not part of a larger unity that would constitute art. But Lowell is profoundly courageous, and he can accept this limitation.

> Yet why not say what happened?
> Pray for the grace of accuracy
> Vermeer gave to the sun's illumination
> stealing like the tide across a map
> to his girl solid with yearning.

The girl is solid with yearning, as is Lowell, as are we all, and we pray for the grace of accuracy to do what we can with what we are and what we have.

> We are poor passing facts,
> warned by that to give
> each figure in the photograph
> his living name.

But this is not a bleak ending to a poet's last volume. George McFadden sees in *Day by Day* a constant struggle between two opposing views of time: the inferior "snapshot" view and the more significant view wherein time is registered through memory and history. "Epilogue," McFadden suggests, is "a write-off of the 'snapshot' approach, and a recognition that . . . without memory —the dimension of time and life, of identification and meaning— the image is static, fixated, factitious, and unliving. Besides accuracy (sharp immediateness) grace is needed."[60] Although I think that McFadden draws too sharp a distinction here—I think Lowell in this volume deliberately blurs the line between the "snapshot" approach and the urge to fit his memories into some sort of coherent pattern—nevertheless McFadden's comment reminds us that we must not neglect the aesthetic element of this conflict. In an article written in 1974 on John Crowe Ransom, Lowell had this to say about the relation of photography to painting: "[Ransom] knows why we do not come back to a photograph for aesthetic pleasure, no matter how colorful and dramatic, not even if it is of a person loved. We cannot feel, as in paintings, the artist's mothering work of hand and mind. I once asked the master photographer Walker Evans how Vermeer's *View of Delft* . . . differed from a photograph. . . . His answer was Ransom's—art demands the intelligent pain or care behind each speck of brick, each spot of paint."[61]

When Lowell speaks of "the intelligent pain or care" behind the work of art, we are reminded once again of the interdependence of Lowell's life and his art, of the extent to which his memory functioned both as a means of self-examination and as a means to art. In "Shifting Colors" (*DBD* 119), the poet himself meditates on these dual functions of memory. In this poem, despite the poet's insistence that he is "too weak to strain to remember," he sees

horse and meadow, duck and pond,
universal consolatory
description without significance,
transcribed verbatim by my eye.

Here "description without significance" is "universal consolatory," and the absence of punctuation merges the individual facts and images into a universal "consolatory" that somehow functions as a noun rather than an adjective and therefore becomes a thing that can allow multiplicities to retain their diversity and yet be part of a "consolatory" whole. Here it is not the poet who is large, who contains multitudes, but rather the world as "transcribed verbatim" by the poet. But more often in *Day by Day* we are acutely aware of that poet, and of "the tenacity with which the aging consciousness seeks to salvage what it can from the past."[62] Lowell returns again and again to the past in this volume, and seems to salvage from his memories not a tidy and completed story, but rather miscellaneous fragments that are sometimes painful but nevertheless, as a whole, "universal consolatory."

Unlike the stereotype of the man who lives more and more in his memory as he gets older, Lowell seems rather to have attained

a nice balance here between the power of the past and the fresh-
ness of "The Day" (*DBD* 53).

> It's amazing
> the day is still here
> like lightning on an open field,
> terra firma and transient
> swimming in variation,
> fresh as when man first broke
> like the crocus all over the earth.

After the turmoil of all the long life and the poetry, "It's amazing /
the day is still here." And this is not just a day but "the" day.
Adam is here, transmuted into "man," but here in all his freshness
and glory and the particularity of the crocus. The rhythm of the
lines, swimming in variation, conveys the exhilaration of the open
field. All oppositions are embraced within these lines: the solid
four stresses in each of the last two lines bring us down to terra
firma, but at the same time the lilt that resists the seriousness of
the four-stress last line releases us into variation again. And mean-
while assonance holds the stanza together and encourages us to
see the unity in the multiplicity.

From intense concentration on the open field of the present, the
poem moves abruptly to the past.

> From a train, we saw cows
> strung out on a hill
> at differing heights,
> one sex, one herd,
> replicas in hierarchy—
> the sun had turned
> them noonday bright.

This is a puzzling interlude; it resists the reader's urge to pin it
down. The "we" does not trouble us, we know that this section
of *Day by Day* is dedicated "To Caroline," and, besides, we know
that the "I"s and "we"s—like Lowell's forebears long ago in *Lord
Weary's Castle*—tend to assume a significance that transcends any
particular identity. But why this particular scene? Why cows?

What in the first section of the poem prepares the poet or the reader for this view from a train?

The immediacy of the image, for one thing: the cows, noonday bright from the sun, embody the same opposing qualities of sameness and difference as does the earth, "terra firma and transient." "One sex, one herd," the cows nevertheless are "strung out on a hill / at differing heights." They are "replicas in hierarchy." And we might attribute the progression of images here to Lowell's associational method as well, as the next lines make clear. Why cows?

> They were child's daubs in a book
> I read before I could read.

Now we can perceive the movement of the poem. The poet begins in the freshness of the present, and then, as he has done over and over in so many of his poems, he returns to his past. The journey here is unsystematic, unforced, the product of seemingly random associations. The poet remembers his childhood and, indeed, what seems at first to be an Eden of oneness with the world, of baby still securely bound to mother, of lover united with lover:

> They fly by like a train window:
> flash-in-the-pan moments
> of the Great Day,
> the *dies illa*,
> when we lived momently
> together forever
> in love with our nature—

The words "momently" and "forever," however, capture the tension implicit in the poem. Although these sensations of union are glorious and all-encompassing, not to be denigrated in any way, nonetheless they exist not on a continuum, not as part of a sustained and coherent narrative or vision, but instead as "flash-in-the-pan moments," fierce but fleeting: the dark spaces that separate the windows of the rushing train car cause the vision to be discontinuous, fragmented. Unlike the journey in "Beyond the Alps" (*LS* 3), which begins quite emphatically in Rome and continues on its linear track to Paris, this journey dissolves, and time and space and life and death combine and coexist.

On the back of one of the drafts of "The Day" is a handwritten list of Lowell's hospitalizations from 1949 to 1974.[63] His list takes the form of a column, and he adds up the number of months spent in hospitals incorrectly. One of the drafts of the poem includes these lines:

In the end
the healthy cannot enter heaven;
in the end
the most bloodless, commissioned biography
has compassion on its subject
and rejoices the heart with tragedy—
in the marriage of nothingness.

To have compassion on the subject and to rejoice the heart with tragedy—these are the great accomplishments of Lowell's poetry of memory. His great subject was, of course, himself, and through himself, all of us. His were rare feats, accomplished through his "one life, one writing" ("Night Sweat," FTUD 68). What his life taught him was that when the intensity of the present moment or the moment glimpsed in memory faded, when the reality of the life threatened, a solution might be found in the mind, in the always-available "as if." "The Day" ends with lines that are characteristic of Lowell, lines that, as Robert Pinsky said of many of the lines in History, mean "a little more than anything the reader can put his finger on, or something a little different."[64] These lines need to be read very slowly, with a definite pause before the last word:

as if in the end
in the marriage with nothingness,
we could ever escape
being absolutely safe.

Afterword:
The Language
of the Self

WHETHER ANSWERS to the great questions of
life are to be found within the individual is a matter to be ad-
dressed by religion and philosophy, but Robert Lowell, like the
Puritans, knew that no matter where truth may lie, the search for
it must be conducted within the self. Lowell's unrelenting search
for self, as it comes to us through his poetry, was conducted par-
tially by means of techniques used in psychoanalysis. And to what
avail was this painful process? "Lowell's commitment to a psychi-
atric concept of health, though genuine, is limited (like Freud's) by
a tragic view of life," Alan Williamson points out. "There is no
universally accepted answer—indeed, there is heated dispute—on
the question of whether analysis can lead only to a livable compro-
mise between the individual and his background, or the reality
principle . . . or whether it can produce a truly free man."[1]

There is some evidence to show that Lowell's life was easier to
bear in his later years. To Steven Gould Axelrod, "the overriding
theme" of Day by Day seems to be "the power of the individual,
despite age and illness, to bear his life, to learn to understand
and even prize it."[2] Alan Williamson tells of the "serenity and
ease" that seemed to "radiate" from Lowell the last time the two
were together.[3] And Day by Day, despite occasional moments of
depression and even despair, reflects a sense of that serenity and
ease. Of course this serenity, however limited, was achieved only
through great struggle, a fact that perhaps helps to explain why

many readers, knowing all the reasons why one might choose not to admire the Robert Lowell who appears in the poetry, nevertheless find him heroic. Anthony Hecht ends an essay on Lowell with a reference to Keats's remark that "a Man's life of any worth is a continual allegory—and very few eyes can see the Mystery of his life—a life like the scriptures, figurative—which such people can no more make out than they can the hebrew Bible. . . . Shakespeare led a life of Allegory; his works are the comments on it." And Hecht applies Keats's definition to Lowell: "through his constant moral and artistic endeavor to situate himself in the midst of our representative modern crises, both personal and political, he has led, for us—as it were, in our behalf—a life of Allegory; and his works are comments on it."[4]

Speaking to an interviewer in 1961 about his "last poems"—presumably those in *Life Studies*, and some in *For the Union Dead*—Lowell had this to say:

> My last poems don't use religious imagery, they don't use symbolism. In many ways they seem to me more religious than the early ones, which are full of symbols and references to Christ and God. . . . Yet I don't feel my experience changed very much. It seems to me it's clearer to me now than it was then, but it's very much the same sort of thing that went into the religious poems—the same sort of struggle, light and darkness, the flux of experience. The morality seems much the same.[5]

Lowell would have been most uncomfortable in the role of lawgiver or moral example, and we must be careful not to cast him in such a limited and limiting part, but when he refers to the "morality" of his poems, I think we should pay attention. When Blair Clark spoke of the "moral function" of Lowell's prep school "miniphalanx," of their commitment to "unmerciful self-scrutiny," he unknowingly repeated the argument of Philip Rieff's *Freud: The Mind of the Moralist:* that "knowing . . . is itself a primary ethical act."[6] In the preface to the first edition of his book, Rieff says that "I have tried to show the mind of Freud . . . as it derives lessons on the right conduct of life from the misery of living it."[7] Readers of Lowell's poetry find that he, too, by the example of his life and

writing, proposes certain moral imperatives which, not coinciden-
tally, are implicit in the process of psychoanalysis. Herbert Leibo-
witz quotes Perry Miller as saying that Jonathan Edwards "was a
Puritan who would not permit mankind to evade the unending
ordeal and the continuing agony of liberty," and Leibowitz adds
"so is Lowell."[8] But Lowell did not ask of humankind any more
than he demanded of himself, in "this life too long for comfort
and too brief / for perfection" ("Long Summer 15," N 31). In a
letter to Pound, he wrote:

> I suppose all young men get up the nerve to start moving by
> wrapping themselves like mummies from nose to toe in col-
> ored cloths, veils, dreams, etc. After a while shedding one's
> costume, one's fancy dress, is like being flayed. I've just been
> doing a little piece of [sic] *Why I live in Boston*. I made it imper-
> sonal and said nothing about what I was looking for here—
> the pain and jolt of seeing things as they are.[9]

Rieff, quoting Freud, tells us that honesty is " 'the fundamental
rule of the psychoanalytic technique.' But what appears as a rule
of therapy is actually a general cultural recommendation."[10] Low-
ell demands of himself honesty—that he not evade or cover up or
shrink from "the pain and jolt of seeing things as they are."[11]

And he demands discipline, and attention to duty. Elizabeth
Hardwick describes his routine shortly after his return from one
period of hospitalization: "Cal was not the sort of poet, if there are
any, for whom beautiful things come drifting down in a snowfall
of gift, the labor was merciless. The discipline, the dedication, the
endless adding to his *store*, by reading and studying—all of this
had, in my view, much that was heroic about it."[12] Lowell de-
mands this kind of heroism, along with the "courage that takes
whatever comes" ("The Vanity of Human Wishes," after Juvenal,
NTO 51). And always he demands of himself that he question,
that he search, explore, that he ferret out the secrets of life:

> Essentially this is how he must always be remembered, one
> moment playful to the point of violent provocation, the next
> in profound contemplation of the great mystery: What does
> life mean? What is it all about? Or, in retrospect and more

accurately for him it is but one moment. As poet, as man, he approaches the great mystery playfully and seriously at the same time.[13]

Readers of Lowell's poems may wish that a little more of the playfulness had entered the poetry—in his "Afterthought" to *Notebook*, Lowell admits, "In truth, I seem to have felt mostly the joys of living; in remembering, in recording, thanks to the gift of the Muse, it is the pain." But even through the pain, an occasional lightness creeps in. While writing his autobiographical sketches in the middle 1950s, Lowell "learned how to give voice to a wide range of what might be called the moderate emotions: affection, regret, nostalgia, embarrassment, and so on"; some of the *Life Studies* poems in particular reflect these "moderate emotions."[14] But, for the most part, it is the serious and "profound contemplation of the great mystery" that we encounter in Lowell's poems and that we admire.

In "New England and Further," an unfinished essay that Lowell began in the late 1960s and put aside until shortly before his death, he speaks of "a longing in New England so strong for what is not that what is not perhaps exists. Or maybe something still deeper, a peculiar stain or genius that is unkillable, inescapable." Here he is describing the New England of the present day, but as is so often the case in his poetry, thoughts of the present lead immediately to thoughts of the past. "Spirit, not powder and character, made the shot fired at Concord heard round the world. This spirit is of the soul, oh, intensely, and it was like an ax that drove the splintered bodies of the first settlers through the splintered wilderness, drove them until they made God in its image."[15]

Lowell's spirit too was of the soul, oh, intensely. "The line must terminate," he said in "Fishnet" (*D* 15): "Yet my heart rises, I know I've gladdened a lifetime / knotting, undoing a fishnet of tarred rope." If we borrow from Robert Graves the metaphor of the web of language, we can see that Lowell indeed spent his lifetime "knotting" and "undoing" the fishnet of language—a carefully constructed net which, though full of holes, enabled him to capture and examine aspects of his self.[16] "Fishnet," the first poem in *The Dolphin*, begins with the words "Any clear thing that blinds us with surprise," and Lowell was able, through his poetry, to reach the occasional "moments of surprise" that Meredith Skura calls "the characteristic marks of a good analysis":[17]

> Like this, like this, as the great clock clangs round,
> I see me—a green hunter who leaps from turn to turn,
> a new brass bugle slung on his invisible baldric;
> he is groping for trout in the private river,
> wherever it opens, wherever it happens to open.
>   ["The Serpent," D 18][18]

Lowell reveled in his moments of surprise, but much of his life had to be spent in the intervals between those moments, examining his self, living his life, writing his poetry. He found in the process no absolutes or certainty, but tentative, day-by-day answers to the questions of our common existence: "How will the hands be strong? How will the heart endure?" ("Mr. Edwards and the Spider," LWC 64).

Notes

Introduction

1. Quoted in Hamilton, *Robert Lowell*, pp. 21–22.
2. Franklin, "Account of My Life," pp. 71–85.
3. Emerson, "Journal 1826," p. 29.
4. Perry Miller, *New England Mind*, pp. 53, 56.
5. Bercovitch, *Puritan Origins*, pp. 18–19.
6. Morgan, *Visible Saints*, p. 113. Because these spiritual "relations," as they were called, were intended to persuade church members of the applicant's "visible sainthood," they tend to de-emphasize the element of struggle so prominent in some of the journals and poetry of the time. For a valuable study of these relations, see Caldwell, *Puritan Conversion Narrative*.
7. Leibowitz, "Ancestral Voices," p. 27.
8. Perry Miller, *New England Mind*, p. 7.
9. Lowell, "Interview with Seidel," p. 240.
10. Lowell, letter to Santayana, 12 January 1948, Santayana Collection.
11. Staples, *Robert Lowell*, p. 99.
12. Perry Miller, *New England Mind*, p. 50. For discussions of the role self-examination plays in the culture and literature of the United States, see Lears, *No Place of Grace*; and Bellah, Madsen, Sullivan, Swidler, and Tipton, *Habits of the Heart*, pp. 55–84.
13. Waelder, *Theory of Psychoanalysis*, p. x.
14. Freud, "Difficulty," 17:143.
15. Leavy, *Psychoanalytic Dialogue*, p. 51.

16. Hamilton, *Robert Lowell*, p. 201.

17. Lowell to Tate, 2 December 1953, Tate Collection.

18. Lowell to Williamson, 23 September 1974. I would like to thank Alan Williamson for sending me a copy of this letter and permitting me to quote sections of it. Because Lowell's spelling and punctuation were often erratic, and because I quote his letters for their sense rather than for felicity of expression, I have here and throughout "corrected" typographical errors in the letters.

19. Alvarez, "Talk with Robert Lowell," pp. 40–41.

20. Ian Hamilton says that although Lowell had several "brushes with analysts"—his therapist for several years in the 1960s was more "analytically inclined" than his former therapists—"he had never 'gone into analysis' " (*Robert Lowell*, pp. 284, 358).

21. Stafford, "Influx of Poets," p. 44.

22. The information in this and the next paragraph comes from Hamilton, *Robert Lowell*, pp. 28, 42, 66, 200.

23. Moore, *M*, n.p. Reprinted at the back of *M* are laudatory remarks on Moore's sonnets by, among others, William Carlos Williams, who says that "Merrill Moore's sonnets are magnificent. . . . If sonnets of importance can now again be written, it is Merrill Moore who has made them possible" (n.p.).

24. Lowell to Santayana, 22 December 1949, Santayana Collection.

25. Lowell to Winslow, 16 January 1956, Lowell Collection, Houghton Library.

26. Lowell to Winslow, 15 March 1958, ibid.

27. Lowell to Williamson.

28. Giroux, Introduction, pp. xiii–xiv.

29. Vendler, "Intractable Metal," p. 126.

30. Bettelheim, *Freud*, pp. 4, 76.

31. Pearson, "Robert Lowell," p. 31.

32. Hamilton, *Robert Lowell*, p. 220. For an account of the evolution of the prose reminiscences, see Breslin, "Robert Lowell," p. 122.

33. Lowell, "Near the Unbalanced Aquarium," p. 362.

34. Rieff, *Freud*, p. 123.

35. Williamson, *Pity the Monsters*, pp. 5–6.

36. Ibid., p. 68.

37. Skura, *Literary Use*, p. 5.

38. Fenichel, *Psychoanalytic Theory*, p. 26. I am not confining my use of the word "ego" in this book to Freud's narrow definition; I use the word in its contemporary, broader sense.

39. Skura, *Literary Use*, pp. 203–4, 208.

40. Sarton, *Mrs. Stevens*, p. 108.
41. Kris, *Psychoanalytic Explorations*, pp. 253–54.
42. Martin, *Robert Lowell*, p. 29.
43. Perloff, *Poetic Art*, p. 48.
44. Hass, "Lowell's Graveyard," p. 59.
45. Pearson, "Robert Lowell," p. 27.
46. Axelrod, *Robert Lowell*, pp. 115–16.
47. Simon, "Abuse of Privilege," p. 545–46.
48. Crick, *Robert Lowell*, p. 126.
49. Williamson, "Robert Lowell," p. 39.
50. Ehrenpreis, "Age of Lowell," p. 86.
51. Prunty, "Allegory to Causality," p. 101.
52. Skura, *Literary Use*, p. 21.
53. Lowell to Winslow, 8 March 1956, Lowell Collection, Houghton Library.
54. Quoted in Hamilton, *Robert Lowell*, p. 417.
55. Ibid., pp. 36–37.
56. Freud, "Lay Analysis," 20:195–96.
57. Pearson, "Robert Lowell," pp. 30–31.
58. Williamson, *Pity the Monsters*, p. 56.
59. Rosenthal, *New Poets*, p. 16.
60. Loewald, "Therapeutic Action," p. 30.
61. Skura, *Literary Use*, p. 73.
62. Waelder, *Theory of Psychoanalysis*, p. 213.
63. Fenichel, *Psychoanalytic Theory*, p. 20.
64. Rieff, *Freud*, p. 28.
65. Taylor, "Lowell 1917–1977," p. 77.
66. Kunitz, "Talk with Robert Lowell," p. 54.
67. Williamson, *Pity the Monsters*, p. 12.
68. Fein, *Robert Lowell*, pp. 170–71. Stephen Yenser says that in terms of poetic method, "the difference is that between one which synthesizes or unites contraries and one which analyzes or insists upon distinctions" (*Circle to Circle*, p. 88). And speaking of *The Mills of the Kavanaughs*, Yenser refers to "Lowell's increased tendency to contradict himself, to get the process of thought rather than its product into the poetry" (p. 83).
69. Axelrod, *Robert Lowell*, p. 54. Compare Perry Miller's remark, quoted earlier, that the Puritans "universalized their own neurasthenia."
70. Jarrell, "Kingdom of Necessity," p. 188.
71. Carruth, "Meaning of Robert Lowell," p. 447.
72. Lowell, "Essays on Me," p. 113. This element of process ("a continuing story—still wayfaring") has struck reader after reader.

M. L. Rosenthal: "his object is to catch himself in process of be-
coming himself" (*New Poets*, p. 28). Neil Corcoran: "poetry as pro-
cess, not realization" ("Lowell *Retiarius*," p. 78). Gabriel Pearson:
the "materials of his own life are there to be made over to art.
Interest focuses on that process, not on the life itself" ("Robert
Lowell," p. 4).

73. Gallop, *Reading Lacan*, p. 83.

74. Jay Martin speaks of Lowell's "inner sense of not holding
together" and "his experience of self-fragmentation" ("Grief and
Nothingness," p. 29). Lawrence Kramer refers to the "dissolution
of the ego" in *Life Studies*, and notes that "the ideal of an inte-
grated, self-affirming ego—the darling of ego psychology—tends
to recede into a mobile, fragmentary, volatile subjectivity" ("Freud
and the Skunks," p. 87). We will discuss the question of the tenta-
tive nature of the self in chapter 4.

75. Altieri, "Sensibility, Rhetoric, and Will," p. 454. Malkoff, *Es-
cape from the Self*, p. 116.

76. Lacan, "Function and Field," p. 49. Schafer, *Narrative Ac-
tions*. Janet Malcolm refers to the "misconception . . . that psycho-
analysis is a sort of cure by narrative" ("J'Appelle un Chat un
Chat," pp. 100–101).

77. Martin, "Grief and Nothingness," p. 30.

78. Freud, "Outline of Psycho-Analysis," 23:205.

Chapter One

1. Lowell to Santayana, 5 January 1949, Santayana Collection.
Compare these lines from "Hawthorne" (*FTUD* 38):

Follow its lazy main street lounging
from the alms house to Gallows Hill
along a flat, unvaried surface
covered with wooden houses
aged by yellow drain
like the unhealthy hair of an old dog.
You'll walk to no purpose
in Hawthorne's Salem.

2. Lacan, "Function and Field," p. 41.
3. Freud, "Five Lectures," 11:32.
4. Quoted in Hamilton, *Robert Lowell*, p. 36.
5. Lowell, draft entitled "The Balanced Aquarium," Lowell Col-

lection, Houghton Library. Compare "Near the Unbalanced Aquarium," pp. 346–47.

6. Silberman, " 'Confessional' Poetry," pp. 126–27. Silberman discusses Lowell's use of psychoanalysis as well.

7. Thomas Clark, "Allen Ginsberg," p. 17.

8. Kerouac, "Spontaneous Prose," p. 72.

9. Ibid., p. 73.

10. Breton, "What Is Surrealism?" pp. 120–21.

11. Freud, "Interpretation of Dreams," 4:102.

12. Breton, "What Is Surrealism?" p. 122.

13. Williamson, *Pity the Monsters*, pp. 158–59.

14. Mark Rudman has a helpful reading of this poem in *Robert Lowell*, pp. 170–73.

15. Freud, "New Introductory Lectures," 22:20.

16. Trilling, "Freud and Literature," p. 53.

17. Freud, "Interpretation of Dreams," 4:247.

18. Ibid., 4:103.

19. Martin, *Robert Lowell*, p. 23.

20. McCormick, "Falling Asleep," p. 272.

21. Hass, "Lowell's Graveyard," p. 65.

22. Perloff, *Poetic Art*, p. 109.

23. Leavy, *Psychoanalytic Dialogue*, pp. 89–90.

24. Perloff, *Poetic Art*, pp. 86–87. See also Lensing, "Associative Mirror," pp. 23–26.

25. Jakobson and Halle, *Fundamentals of Language*, p. 92. Jacques Lacan has developed and extended Jakobson's theory. See, for example, Wilden, "Lacan and Discourse," pp. 238–49.

26. Kerouac, "Spontaneous Prose," p. 72.

27. Reik, *Listening with the Third Ear*, p. 29. Compare the "composition of place," the first step in the process of meditation prescribed by Ignatius Loyola and widely practiced in the Renaissance. The subject begins by meditating on an object or on a specific memory, and from there he moves into the meditation itself. In Louis Martz's *The Poetry of Meditation*, which describes poetry based on this process, the frontispiece shows a Hamlet-like youth gazing at a skull. And in *The Continuity of American Poetry*, Roy Harvey Pearce describes the Puritan poet Edward Taylor's use of a similar process of meditation. Speaking of the Puritan Thomas Hooker's description of the process of self-examination, Pearce infers that a "man may will himself to meditate; but he cannot plan. He must take things as they come. The order is theirs, not his" (p. 43).

28. Yenser, *Circle to Circle*, p. 221.

29. Williamson, *Pity the Monsters*, p. 8.
30. Hass, "Lowell's Graveyard," pp. 58–59.
31. Williamson, *Pity the Monsters*, p. 11.
32. Kramer, "Freud and the Skunks," pp. 84–85.
33. Williamson, *Pity the Monsters*, pp. 57–58.
34. Hamilton, "Conversation with Robert Lowell," p. 12. In the revised version of this interview that is included in Lowell's *Collected Prose*, the sentence about surrealism is omitted (p. 269).
35. Axelrod, *Robert Lowell*, p. 153. Richard Fein discusses this poem in *Robert Lowell*, pp. 120–23.
36. Compare this description from Lowell's "Near the Unbalanced Aquarium": "The air in the room began to tighten around me. I felt as if I were squatting on the bottom of a huge laboratory bottle and trying to push out the black rubber stopper before I stifled" (p. 352). In this prose piece, Lowell is describing one of his stays at the Payne-Whitney Clinic of New York Hospital.
37. Parkinson, *"For the Union Dead,"* p. 91. In his "Essay on the Uncanny," Freud relates the idea of the double to the split between the observing and the experiencing self (17:235). See also Anthony Wilden's discussion of the relation of the alter ego or double to Lacan's celebrated "mirror stage" of development, which is in part the subject of chapter 4 of this book (Wilden, "Lacan and Discourse," pp. 164–65).
38. Lowell to Tate, 9 October 1964, Tate Collection. As Axelrod, among others, has pointed out, the poem seems indebted even more clearly to Tate's "The Buried Lake" (*Robert Lowell*, p. 153).
39. Alan Holder discusses this same point in "Going Back," p. 159.
40. McFadden, "Prose or This," pp. 235, 232. Although McFadden confines his discussion of interrelated images to *Day by Day*, his comments can be extended as well to the body of Lowell's poetry.
41. Lowell, Comments on "Bringing a Turtle Home."
42. Cooper, *Autobiographical Myth*, p. 96.
43. McFadden, "Prose or This," p. 235.
44. Axelrod, *Robert Lowell*, p. 234.
45. Lowell, "On 'Skunk Hour,' " p. 228.
46. Simpson, "Robert Lowell's Indissoluble Bride," p. 148.
47. Lowell, "Interview with Seidel," p. 266.

Chapter Two

1. Freud, "Remembering, Repeating and Working-Through," 12:150.
2. Freud, "Essay on the Uncanny," 17:238. Neil Hertz, in "Freud and the Sandman," discusses Freud's association of the uncanny with the repetition compulsion (pp. 296–321). And see Sacvan Bercovitch's discussion of the Puritans' " 'Self Civil War'—as they repeatedly describe the struggle—of a Puritan Sisyphus, driven by self-loathing to Christ and forced back to himself" over and over again (*Puritan Origins*, p. 19).
3. Laplanche and Pontalis, *Language of Psychoanalysis*, p. 78.
4. See Irwin, *Doubling and Incest*, esp. pp. 74–122.
5. Yenser, *Circle to Circle*, p. 4.
6. Ibid., pp. 41–56. Williamson, *Pity the Monsters*, pp. 47–58.
7. Freud, "Analysis of a Phobia," 10:122.
8. Williamson, *Pity the Monsters*, p. 54.
9. Hamilton, *Robert Lowell*, p. 69.
10. Jarrell, "Kingdom of Necessity," pp. 193–94.
11. Yenser, *Circle to Circle*, p. 312. Discussing "Christmas Eve under Hooker's Statue" (*LWC* 23), James E. B. Breslin says that in this poem "history . . . is repetition" ("Robert Lowell," p. 115).
12. Hass, "Lowell's Graveyard," pp. 65–66.
13. Berryman, "Despondency and Madness," pp. 99, 100, 104.
14. Lowell, "On 'Skunk Hour,' " p. 226.
15. Kunitz, "Sense of a Life," p. 43. When I first typed this quotation, I wrote "forever tinkering with his old lives" instead of "forever tinkering with his old lines."
16. McCormick, "Falling Asleep," p. 274.
17. David Kalstone has remarked, "Perhaps no poet since Whitman has made such continuous public revisions of his life. Yet Whitman accumulated everything he wrote into *Leaves of Grass*, as a way of making his book coterminous with his life; it would end only when he did. Lowell, on the contrary, performed a series of amputations and separations" ("Robert Lowell," pp. 66–67).
18. Fein, *Robert Lowell*, p. 168.
19. Kunitz, "Sense of a Life," p. 42.
20. Melville, *Moby-Dick*, pp. 422–23.
21. Freud, "Pleasure Principle," 18:15, 17.
22. Fenichel, *Psychoanalytic Theory*, p. 19.
23. Bibrung, "Repetition Compulsion," pp. 487, 488, 501–2, 498.
24. Laplanche and Pontalis, *Language of Psychoanalysis*, p. 488.
25. Martin, *Robert Lowell*, p. 11, my emphasis.

26. Fenichel, *Psychoanalytic Theory*, p. 31, my emphasis.

27. Leavy, *Psychoanalytic Dialogue*, pp. 99–100.

28. J. Hillis Miller, *Fiction and Repetition*, p. 6.

29. Riddell, "Decentering the Image," p. 357.

30. See Eileen Simpson, *Poets in Their Youth*. "Despondency and madness" is a quotation borrowed by Lowell from Wordsworth and deliberately misused in "To Delmore Schwartz" (*LS* 53).

31. Kalstone has a helpful discussion of the "rebellion" poems ("Robert Lowell," pp. 45–48).

32. Staples, *Robert Lowell*, p. 17.

33. Robert Hass says of this poem that its "stresses falling like chains clanking" seem "to accuse not only the fathers but the culture that produced meter and rhyme" ("One Body," p. 338).

34. Lowell's dramatization of Hawthorne's "My Kinsman, Major Molineux" depicts a similar dreamlike, symbolic rebellion.

35. Nims, *Western Wind*, p. 191.

36. Staples, *Robert Lowell*, p. 17.

37. Yenser, *Circle to Circle*, pp. 73–74.

38. Eliot, "Little Gidding," p. 143.

39. Jarrell, "Kingdom of Necessity," pp. 188, 190.

40. Fein, *Robert Lowell*, p. 91.

41. Axelrod, *Robert Lowell*, p. 68.

42. Malkoff, *Escape from the Self*, p. 121.

43. Kawin, *Telling It Again and Again*, p. 4. Robert B. Shaw has remarked that, in *Day by Day*, Lowell's "renewed attention to subjects he had treated in past books surprisingly avoids repetitiveness." Shaw is of course using not Kawin's but a more common definition of the word "repetitive" ("Lowell in the Seventies," p. 524).

Chapter Three

1. Lacan, "Function and Field," p. 40.

2. See Kris, *Psychoanalytic Explorations*, p. 254.

3. Alvarez, "Robert Lowell in Conversation," p. 38.

4. In Terrence Doody's view, "Confession has a deliberate, formal intention which includes the confessor in the nature of the act." A confession is "the deliberate, self-conscious attempt of an individual to explain his nature to the audience who represents the kind of community he needs to exist in and to confirm him"

57. McClatchy, "Photographs of Lowell," p. 29.

58. The conflict is evident in the sonnets Lowell wrote obsessively for so long, sonnets which, as McClatchy says, are "lyric episodes, contained glimpses. They accumulate rather than narrate, and will always be at odds with epic's traditional dramatic storytelling. The risk is that they are accumulated fragments and won't cohere" ("Photographs of Lowell," p. 241). Lowell himself acknowledged, in response to a question as to whether he found the sonnet form constricting, "Formlessness might have crowded me toward consecutive narrative" ("Conversation with Hamilton," p. 271).

59. Lowell, drafts of "Epilogue," Lowell Collection, Ransom Humanities Research Center.

60. McFadden, "Prose or This," p. 252.

61. Lowell, "John Crowe Ransom," p. 27. Helen Deese has an interesting discussion of Svetlana Alpers's distinction between "descriptive" and "narrative" art, and its relation to Lowell's poetry ("Lowell and the Visual Arts," pp. 184–85).

62. Shaw, "Lowell in the Seventies," p. 526.

63. Lowell, drafts of "The Day," Lowell Collection, Ransom Humanities Research Center.

64. Pinsky, "Conquered Kings," pp. 104–5.

Afterword

1. Williamson, *Pity the Monsters*, pp. 68–69.

2. Axelrod, *Robert Lowell*, p. 235. Marjorie Perloff maintains that in his final years Lowell "seems to have attained the self-knowledge he had always been seeking" ("Holding Back Nothing," p. 104).

3. Williamson, "Robert Lowell," p. 39.

4. Hecht, "Robert Lowell," p. 289.

5. Lowell, "Interview with Seidel," p. 250.

6. Rieff, *Freud*, p. 322.

7. Ibid., p. ix.

8. Leibowitz, "Robert Lowell," p. 42.

9. Quoted in Hamilton, *Robert Lowell*, p. 221.

10. Rieff, *Freud*, p. 316.

11. Compare Perry Miller: "Puritanism . . . demanded that the individual confront existence directly on all sides at once, that he test all things by the touchstone of absolute truth, that no allow-

ance be made for circumstances or for human frailty. . . . It demanded unblinking perception of the facts, though they should slay us" (*New England Mind*, p. 45).

12. Quoted in Hamilton, *Robert Lowell*, p. 258.

13. Taylor, "Lowell 1917–1977," p. 75.

14. Hamilton, *Robert Lowell*, p. 232.

15. Lowell, "New England and Further," pp. 180–81.

16. Graves, "The Cool Web." In an essay on John Berryman, Lowell tells of having briefly imitated the young Berryman's style when the two were together at Damariscotta Mills, Maine. But "nets so grandly knotted could only catch logs—our first harsh, inarticulate cry of truth" ("John Berryman," p. 112).

17. Skura, *Literary Use*, p. 204.

18. Meredith Skura has pointed out to me the Shakespearean echoes in this passage. Benedick, in *Much Ado About Nothing* (I.i.240–42), uses "hang my bugle in an invisible baldrick" as a reference to cuckoldry; Pompey, the clown in *Measure for Measure* (I.ii.90), uses "groping for trouts in a peculiar river" as a reference to sexual intercourse.

Bibliography

Manuscript Sources

Austin, Texas
Harry Ransom Humanities Research Center, University of Texas
at Austin. By permission of the Harry Ransom Humanities Re-
search Center.
  Robert Lowell Collection
    Lowell, Robert. Drafts of "The Day."
    _____. Drafts of "Epilogue."
    _____. Drafts of "Ulysses and Circe."
  George Santayana Collection
    Lowell, Robert. Letter to George Santayana. 12 January 1948.
    _____. Letter to George Santayana. 5 January 1949.
    _____. Letter to George Santayana. 22 December 1949.

Cambridge, Massachusetts
Houghton Library, Harvard University. By permission of the
Houghton Library.
  Robert Lowell Collection
    Lowell, Robert. "The Balanced Aquarium" (drafts of "Near
      the Unbalanced Aquarium").
    _____. "John Milton's Prayer." Unpublished poem.
    _____. Letter to Harriet Winslow. 27 December 1955.
    _____. Letter to Harriet Winslow. 16 January 1956.
    _____. Letter to Harriet Winslow. 8 March 1956.
    _____. Letter to Harriet Winslow. 15 March 1958.

Princeton, New Jersey
Princeton University Library. Published with permission of
Princeton University Library.
   Allen Tate Collection
      Lowell, Robert. Letter to Allen Tate. 2 December 1953.
      _____. Letter to Allen Tate. 9 October 1964.

Personal Communication
Lowell, Robert. Letter to Alan Williamson. 23 September 1974. In
Alan Williamson's possession. Used with Alan Williamson's
permission.

Books of Poetry by Robert Lowell

(asterisks indicate volumes cited)
Day by Day. New York: Farrar, Straus & Giroux, 1977. London:
   Faber & Faber, 1978.
The Dolphin. New York: Farrar, Straus & Giroux, 1973. London:
   Faber & Faber, 1973.
For Lizzie and Harriet. New York: Farrar, Straus & Giroux, 1973.
   London: Faber & Faber, 1973.
For the Union Dead. New York: Farrar, Straus & Giroux, 1964. Lon-
   don: Faber & Faber, 1965. *Rpt. with *Life Studies*, New York:
   Noonday–Farrar, Straus & Giroux, 1968.
History. New York: Farrar, Straus & Giroux, 1973. London: Faber
   & Faber, 1973.
Imitations. New York: Farrar, Straus & Giroux, 1961. London:
   Faber & Faber, 1962.
Land of Unlikeness. Cummington, Mass.: Cummington Press,
   1944. Unpaginated.
Life Studies. New York: Farrar, Straus & Giroux, 1959. London:
   Faber & Faber, 1959. Rpt. New York: Vintage, 1960. *Rpt. with
   For the Union Dead, New York: Noonday–Farrar, Straus &
   Giroux, 1968.
Lord Weary's Castle. New York: Harcourt, Brace and Co., 1946.
   *Rpt. with *The Mills of the Kavanaughs*, New York: Harcourt
   Brace Jovanovich, 1974.
The Mills of the Kavanaughs. New York: Harcourt, Brace and Co.,
   1951. *Rpt. with *Lord Weary's Castle*, New York: Harcourt Brace
   Jovanovich, 1974.
Near the Ocean. New York: Farrar, Straus & Giroux, 1967. London:
   Faber & Faber, 1967.

Notebook. 3d ed., rev. and expanded, New York: Farrar, Straus & Giroux, 1970. London: Faber & Faber, 1970.

Notebook 1967–68. New York: Farrar, Straus & Giroux, 1969.

Poems 1938–1949. London: Faber & Faber, 1950.

Robert Lowell's Poems: A Selection. Edited by Jonathan Raban. London: Faber & Faber, 1974.

Selected Poems. London: Faber & Faber, 1965.

Selected Poems. Rev. ed. New York: Farrar, Straus & Giroux, 1977.

Other Works by and about Robert Lowell

(asterisks indicate volumes cited)

Altieri, Charles. "Sensibility, Rhetoric, and Will: Some Tensions in Contemporary Poetry." *Contemporary Literature* 23 (Fall 1982): 451–79.

Alvarez, A. "Robert Lowell in Conversation." *The Review,* no. 8 (August 1963): 36–40. Rpt. as "Robert Lowell in Conversation II" in *Profile of Robert Lowell,* edited by Jerome Mazzaro, 36–40. Columbus, Ohio: Charles E. Merrill, 1971.

_____. "A Talk with Robert Lowell." *Encounter* 24 (February 1965): 39–43. Rpt. in *Profile of Robert Lowell,* edited by Jerome Mazzaro, 40–48. Columbus, Ohio: Charles E. Merrill, 1971.

Axelrod, Steven Gould. Letter to author. 30 June 1986.

_____. *Robert Lowell: Life and Art.* Princeton: Princeton University Press, 1978.

Belitt, Ben. "*Imitations:* Translation as Personal Mode." *Salmagundi* 1.4 (1966–67): 44–56. Rpt. in *Robert Lowell: A Portrait of the Artist in His Time,* edited by Michael London and Robert Boyers, 115–29. New York: David Lewis, 1970.

Bell, Vereen M. *Robert Lowell: Nihilist as Hero.* Cambridge, Mass.: Harvard University Press, 1983.

Berryman, John. "Despondency and Madness." In *The Contemporary Poet as Artist and Critic,* edited by Anthony Ostroff, 99–106. Boston: Little, Brown, 1964.

Breslin, James E. B. "Robert Lowell." In *From Modern to Contemporary: American Poetry, 1945–1965,* by James E. B. Breslin, 110–42. Chicago: University of Chicago Press, 1984.

Calder, Alex. "*Notebook 1967–68:* Writing the Process Poem." In *Robert Lowell: Essays on the Poetry,* edited by Steven Gould Axelrod and Helen Deese, 117–38. Cambridge: Cambridge University Press, 1986.

Carruth, Hayden. "A Meaning of Robert Lowell." *Hudson Review*

20 (Autumn 1967): 429–47. Rpt. in *Robert Lowell: A Portrait of the Artist in His Time*, edited by Michael London and Robert Boyers, 222–42. New York: David Lewis, 1970.

Clark, Blair. "On Robert Lowell." *Harvard Advocate: Commemorative to Robert Lowell* (November 1979): 9–11.

Cooper, Philip. *The Autobiographical Myth of Robert Lowell*. Chapel Hill: University of North Carolina Press, 1970.

Corcoran, Neil. "Lowell *Retiarius:* Towards *The Dolphin." Agenda* 18 (Autumn 1980): 75–85.

Crick, John. *Robert Lowell*. New York: Barnes and Noble, 1974.

Deese, Helen. "Lowell and the Visual Arts." In *Robert Lowell: Essays on the Poetry*, edited by Steven Gould Axelrod and Helen Deese, 180–216. Cambridge: Cambridge University Press, 1986.

Ehrenpreis, Irvin. "The Age of Lowell." In **American Poetry* (Stratford upon Avon Studies 7), 69–95. Series edited by John Russell Brown and Bernard Harris. Volume edited by Irvin Ehrenpreis. New York: St. Martin's Press, 1965. Rpt. in *Robert Lowell: A Collection of Critical Essays*, edited by Thomas Parkinson, 74–98. Englewood Cliffs, N.J.: Prentice-Hall, 1968. Rpt. in *Robert Lowell: A Portrait of the Artist in His Time*, edited by Michael London and Robert Boyers, 155–86. New York: David Lewis, 1970. Rpt. as "The Growth of a Poet" in *Critics on Robert Lowell*, edited by Jonathan Price, 15–36. Coral Gables: University of Miami Press, 1972.

Fein, Richard J. *Robert Lowell*. 2d ed. Boston: Twayne Publishers, 1979.

Giroux, Robert. Introduction to *Robert Lowell: Collected Prose*, edited by Robert Giroux, x–xiv. New York: Farrar, Straus & Giroux, 1987.

Hamilton, Ian. "A Conversation with Robert Lowell." **The Review*, no. 26 (Summer 1971): 10–29. Rev. and rpt. as Robert Lowell, "A Conversation with Ian Hamilton." *American Poetry Review* 7 (September–October 1978): 23–27.

———. *Robert Lowell: A Biography*. New York: Random House, 1982.

Hass, Robert. "Lowell's Graveyard." *Salmagundi*, no. 37 (Spring 1977): 56–72.

Hecht, Anthony. "Robert Lowell." In *Obbligati: Essays in Criticism*, by Anthony Hecht, 264–89. New York: Atheneum, 1986.

Holder, Alan. "Going Back, Going Down, Breaking: *Day by Day*." In *Robert Lowell: Essays on the Poetry*, edited by Steven Gould Axelrod and Helen Deese, 156–79. Cambridge: Cambridge University Press, 1986.

Jarrell, Randall. "From the Kingdom of Necessity." In *Poetry and the Age*, 188–99. 1953; *rpt. New York: Vintage, 1959. Rpt. in *Robert Lowell: A Collection of Critical Essays*, edited by Thomas Parkinson, 40–47. Englewood Cliffs, N.J.: Prentice-Hall, 1968. Rpt. in *Robert Lowell: A Portrait of the Artist in His Time*, edited by Michael London and Robert Boyers, 19–27. New York: David Lewis, 1970. Rpt. in *Critics on Robert Lowell*, edited by Jonathan Price, 47–52. Coral Gables: University of Miami Press, 1972.

———. "Three Books." In *Poetry and the Age*, 230–36. 1953; *rpt. New York: Vintage, 1959. Rpt. as *"The Mills of the Kavanaughs"* in *Robert Lowell: A Portrait of the Artist in His Time*, edited by Michael London and Robert Boyers, 38–43. New York: David Lewis, 1970.

Kalstone, David. "Robert Lowell: The Uses of History." In *Five Temperaments*, by David Kalstone, 41–76. New York: Oxford University Press, 1977.

Kramer, Lawrence. "Freud and the Skunks: Genre and Language in *Life Studies*." In *Robert Lowell: Essays on the Poetry*, edited by Steven Gould Axelrod and Helen Deese, 80–98. Cambridge: Cambridge University Press, 1986.

Kunitz, Stanley. "Robert Lowell: The Sense of a Life." In *Next-to-Last Things: New Poems and Essays*, by Stanley Kunitz, 39–49. Boston: Atlantic Monthly Press, 1985.

———. "Talk with Robert Lowell." In *Profile of Robert Lowell*, edited by Jerome Mazzaro, 53–59. Columbus, Ohio: Charles E. Merrill, 1971.

Leibowitz, Herbert. "Robert Lowell: Ancestral Voices." *Salmagundi* 1.4 (1966–67): 25–43. Rpt. in *Robert Lowell: A Portrait of the Artist in His Time*, edited by Michael London and Robert Boyers, 199–221. New York: David Lewis, 1970.

Lensing, George. " 'Memories of West Street and Lepke': Robert Lowell's Associative Mirror." *Concerning Poetry* 3 (Fall 1970): 23–26.

Lieberman, Laurence. "Beyond the Muse of Memory: Robert Lowell's Last Face." *Southwest Review* 71 (Winter 1986): 78–96.

Lowell, Robert. "After Enjoying Six or Seven Essays on Me." *Salmagundi*, no. 37 (Spring 1977): 112–15.

———. *Collected Prose*. Edited by Robert Giroux. New York: Farrar, Straus & Giroux, 1987.

"Antebellum Boston" (1957): 291–308.

"A Conversation with Ian Hamilton" (1971): 267–90.

"For John Berryman, 1914–1972" (1972): 111–18.

"Four Quartets" (1943): 45–48.

"An Interview with Frederick Seidel" (1961): 235–66.

"John Crowe Ransom 1888–1974" (1974): 20–28.

"Near the Unbalanced Aquarium" (1957): 346–63.

"New England and Further" (1977): 179–212.

"On 'Skunk Hour' " (1964): 225–29.

"Dr. Williams" (1962): 37–44.

———. [Comments on "Bringing a Turtle Home" and "Returning Turtle."] In *The Poet's Voice: Poets Reading Aloud and Commenting upon Their Works*, edited by Stratis Haviaras. Cambridge, Mass.: Harvard University Press, 1978.

———. "My Kinsman, Major Molineux." In *The Old Glory*, 81–134. Rev. ed. New York: Farrar, Straus & Giroux, 1968.

McClatchy, J. D. "Some Photographs of Robert Lowell." *American Poetry Review* 7.5 (September–October 1978): 28–29.

McCormick, John. "Falling Asleep over Grillparzer: An Interview with Robert Lowell." *Poetry* 81 (January 1953): 269–79.

McFadden, George. " 'Life Studies'—Robert Lowell's Comic Breakthrough." *PMLA* 90 (January 1975): 96–106.

———. " 'Prose or This': What Lowell Made of a Diminished Thing." In *Robert Lowell: Essays on the Poetry*, edited by Steven Gould Axelrod and Helen Deese, 231–55. Cambridge: Cambridge University Press, 1986.

Malkoff, Karl. *Escape from the Self: A Study in Contemporary American Poetry and Poetics*. New York: Columbia University Press, 1977.

Martin, Jay. "Grief and Nothingness: Loss and Mourning in Lowell's Poetry." In *Robert Lowell: Essays on the Poetry*, edited by Steven Gould Axelrod and Helen Deese, 26–50. Cambridge: Cambridge University Press, 1986.

———. *Robert Lowell*. University of Minnesota Pamphlets on American Writers, no. 92. Minneapolis: University of Minnesota Press, 1970.

Michelson, Bruce. "Lowell versus Lowell." *Virginia Quarterly Review* 59 (Winter 1983): 22–39.

Parkinson, Thomas. "*For the Union Dead*." *Salmagundi* 1.4 (1966–67): 87–95. Rpt. in *Robert Lowell: A Collection of Critical Essays*, edited by Thomas Parkinson, 143–51. Englewood Cliffs, N.J.: Prentice-Hall, 1968.

Pearson, Gabriel. "*For Lizzie and Harriet*: Robert Lowell's Domestic Apocalypse." In *Modern American Poetry*, edited by R. W. (Herbie) Butterfield, 187–203. London: Vision Press; and Totowa, N.J.: Barnes and Noble, 1984.

———. "Lowell's Marble Meanings." In *The Survival of Poetry*, edited by Martin Dodsworth, 56–99. London: Faber & Faber, 1970.

———. "Robert Lowell." *Review*, no. 20 (March 1969): 3–36.

Perloff, Marjorie. " 'Fearlessly Holding Back Nothing': Robert Lowell's Last Poems." *Agenda* 18 (Autumn 1980): 104–13.

———. *The Poetic Art of Robert Lowell.* Ithaca, N.Y.: Cornell University Press, 1973.

Pinsky, Robert. "The Conquered Kings of Robert Lowell." *Salmagundi*, no. 37 (Spring 1977): 102–5.

Poirier, Richard. *"For the Union Dead."* In *Critics on Robert Lowell*, edited by Jonathan Price, 92–96. Coral Gables: University of Miami Press, 1972.

Procopiow, Norma. *Robert Lowell: The Poet and His Critics.* Chicago: American Library Association, 1984.

Prunty, Wyatt. "Allegory to Causality: Robert Lowell's Poetic Shift." *Agenda* 18 (Autumn 1980): 94–103.

Rosenthal, M. L. *The New Poets: American and British Poetry since World War II.* New York: Oxford University Press, 1967.

———. "Robert Lowell and the Poetry of Confession." In *Robert Lowell: A Portrait of the Artist in His Time*, edited by Michael London and Robert Boyers, 44–57. New York: David Lewis, 1970.

Rudman, Mark. *Robert Lowell: An Introduction to the Poetry.* New York: Columbia University Press, 1983.

Shaw, Robert B. "Lowell in the Seventies." *Contemporary Literature* 23 (Fall 1982): 515–27.

Simon, John. "Abuse of Privilege: Lowell as Translator." **Hudson Review* 20 (Winter 1967–68): 543–62. Rpt. in *Robert Lowell: A Portrait of the Artist in His Time*, edited by Michael London and Robert Boyers, 130–51. New York: David Lewis, 1970.

Simpson, Louis. "Robert Lowell's Indissoluble Bride." In *A Revolution in Taste*, by Louis Simpson, 129–67. New York: Macmillan, 1978.

Staples, Hugh B. *Robert Lowell: The First Twenty Years.* London: Faber & Faber, 1962.

Taylor, Peter. "Robert Trail [*sic*] Spence Lowell 1917–1977." *Ploughshares* 5.2 (1979): 74–81.

Tillinghast, Richard. "Reading Through Robert Lowell's Enigmas." *Agenda* 18 (Autumn 1980): 86–93.

Vendler, Helen. "The Poetry of Autobiography." Rev. of *Day by Day*, by Robert Lowell. *New York Times Book Review* (14 August 1977): 1, 24–25.

———. "Pudding Stone." Rev. of *Robert Lowell: Life and Art*, by Steven Gould Axelrod. In *Part of Nature, Part of Us: Modern*

American Poets, by Helen Vendler, 152–61. Cambridge, Mass.: Harvard University Press, 1980.

––––––. "Ulysses, Circe, Penelope." *Salmagundi*, no. 37 (Spring 1977): 16–24.

Wallingford, Katharine. "Robert Lowell and Free Association." *Mosaic* 19.4 (Fall 1986): 121–32.

––––––. "Robert Lowell's Poetry of Repetition." *American Literature* 57 (October 1985): 424–33.

Weatherhead, A. Kingsley. "*Day by Day*: His End Game." In *Robert Lowell: Essays on the Poetry*, edited by Steven Gould Axelrod and Helen Deese, 217–29. Cambridge: Cambridge University Press, 1986.

Williamson, Alan. *Pity the Monsters: The Political Vision of Robert Lowell*. New Haven: Yale University Press, 1974.

––––––. "Robert Lowell: A Reminiscence." *Harvard Advocate: Commemorative to Robert Lowell* (November 1979): 36–39.

Yenser, Stephen. *Circle to Circle: The Poetry of Robert Lowell*. Berkeley: University of California Press, 1975.

Other Sources

Abraham, Karl. "Dreams and Myths: A Study in Folk-Psychology" (1909). In *Clinical Papers and Essays on Psycho-Analysis*. Edited by Hilda C. Abraham, translated by Hilda C. Abraham and D. R. Ellison, with Hilda Maas and Anna Hackel, 153–209. London: The Hogarth Press, 1955.

Bellah, Robert N.; Madsen, Richard; Sullivan, William M.; Swidler, Ann; and Tipton, Steven M. *Habits of the Heart: Individualism and Commitment in American Life*. Berkeley: University of California Press, 1985.

Bercovitch, Sacvan. *The Puritan Origins of the American Self*. New Haven: Yale University Press, 1975.

Bettelheim, Bruno. *Freud and Man's Soul*. 1982; rpt. New York: Vintage, 1984.

Bibrung, Edward. "The Conception of the Repetition Compulsion." *Psychoanalytic Quarterly* 12 (1943): 486–519.

Bishop, Elizabeth. "In the Village." In *Questions of Travel*, 44–47. New York: Farrar, Straus & Giroux, 1965.

Brenkman, John. "Narcissus in the Text." *Georgia Review* 30 (Summer 1976): 293–327.

Breton, André. "What Is Surrealism?" (1934). In *What Is Surrealism?: Selected Writings*, edited by Franklin Rosemont, 112–41.

N.p.: Monad Press, 1978. From an English translation by David Gascoyne. London: Faber & Faber, 1936.

Caldwell, Patricia. *The Puritan Conversion Narrative: The Beginnings of American Expression.* Cambridge: Cambridge University Press, 1983.

Clark, Thomas. "The Art of Poetry VIII: Allen Ginsberg." *Paris Review* 37 (Spring 1966): 13–55.

Doody, Terrence. *Confession and Community in the Novel.* Baton Rouge: Louisiana State University Press, 1980.

Eliot, T. S. "Little Gidding." In *The Complete Poems and Plays, 1909–1950,* 138–45. New York: Harcourt, Brace, 1952.

Emerson, Ralph Waldo. [Journal 1826]. *The Journals and Miscellaneous Notebooks.* 16 vols. Edited by William H. Gilman and Alfred R. Ferguson. Cambridge, Mass.: Belknap Press of Harvard University Press, 1963.

Feidelson, Charles, Jr. *Symbolism and American Literature.* Chicago: University of Chicago Press, 1953.

Fenichel, Otto. *The Psychoanalytic Theory of Neurosis.* New York: Norton, 1945.

Foucault, Michel. "Nietzsche, Genealogy, History" (1971). In *Language, Counter-Memory, Practice: Selected Essays and Interviews,* edited by Donald F. Bouchard, 139–64. Translated by Donald F. Bouchard and Sherry Simon. Ithaca, N.Y.: Cornell University Press, 1977.

Franklin, Benjamin. "Continuation of the Account of My Life, Begun at Passy, 1784" (1784). In *The Autobiography and Other Writings,* edited by Peter Shaw, 71–85. New York: Bantam, 1982.

Freud, Sigmund. *The Standard Edition of the Complete Psychological Works.* 24 vols. Edited and translated by James Strachey and others. London: Hogarth, 1953–74.

"Analysis of a Phobia in a Five-Year-Old Boy" (1909). 10:1–149.

"Beyond the Pleasure Principle" (1920). 18:7–64.

"A Difficulty in the Path of Psycho-Analysis" (1917). 17:135–44.

"Essay on the Uncanny" (1919). 17:217–52.

"Five Lectures on Psycho-Analysis" (1910 [1909]). 11:1–55.

"The Interpretation of Dreams" (1900). 4–5:1–627.

"Moses and Monotheism" (1939 [1934–38]). 23:1–137.

"New Introductory Lectures on Psycho-Analysis" (1933 [1932]). 22:1–182.

"An Outline of Psycho-Analysis" (1940 [1938]). 23:139–207.

"The Question of Lay Analysis" (1926). 20:177–258.

"Remembering, Repeating and Working-Through" (1914). 12:145–56.

"Totem and Taboo" (1913 [1912–13]). 13:1–162.

Gallop, Jane. *Reading Lacan*. Ithaca, N.Y.: Cornell University Press, 1985.

Graves, Robert. "The Cool Web." In *Collected Poems*, 45. Garden City, N.Y.: Doubleday-Anchor, 1966.

Gross, Harvey. *Sound and Form in Modern Poetry*. Ann Arbor: University of Michigan Press, 1964.

Hass, Robert. "Meditation at Lagunitas." In *Praise*, 4–5. New York: Ecco Press, 1979.

———. "One Body: Some Notes on Form." *Antaeus*, no. 30/31 (Spring 1978): 329–42.

Hertz, Neil. "Freud and the Sandman." In *Textual Strategies: Perspectives in Post-Structuralist Criticism*, edited by Josué V. Harari, 296–321. Ithaca, N.Y.: Cornell University Press, 1979.

Irwin, John. *Doubling and Incest / Repetition and Revenge*. Baltimore: Johns Hopkins University Press, 1975.

Jakobson, Roman, and Halle, Morris. *Fundamentals of Language*. 2d ed. The Hague: Mouton, 1971.

Jay, Paul. *Being in the Text: Self-Representation from Wordsworth to Roland Barthes*. Ithaca, N.Y.: Cornell University Press, 1984.

Kawin, Bruce. *Telling It Again and Again: Repetition in Literature and Film*. Ithaca, N.Y.: Cornell University Press, 1972.

Kerouac, Jack. "Essentials of Spontaneous Prose." *Evergreen Review* 2 (Summer 1958): 72–73.

Kris, Ernst. *Psychoanalytic Explorations in Art*. New York: Schocken Books, 1952.

Lacan, Jacques. *The Four Fundamental Concepts of Psycho-Analysis*. Edited by Jacques-Alain Miller. Translated by Alan Sheridan. New York: Norton, 1978.

———. "The Function and Field of Speech and Language in Psychoanalysis" (1953). In *Ecrits: A Selection*, 30–113. Translated by Alan Sheridan. New York: Norton, 1977.

———. "The Mirror Stage as Formative of the Function of the I as Revealed in Psychoanalytic Experience" (1949). In *Ecrits: A Selection*, 1–7. Translated by Alan Sheridan. New York: Norton, 1977.

———. *Speech and Language in Psychoanalysis*. Originally published as *The Language of the Self: The Function of Language in Psychoanalysis*. Translated by Anthony Wilden. Baltimore: Johns Hopkins University Press, 1968.

Laplanche, J., and Pontalis, J.-B. *The Language of Psychoanalysis*.

Translated by Donald Nicholson-Smith. New York: Norton, 1973.

Lears, T. J. Jackson. *No Place of Grace: Antimodernism and the Transformation of American Culture, 1880–1920.* New York: Pantheon Books, 1981.

Leavy, Stanley A. *The Psychoanalytic Dialogue.* New Haven: Yale University Press, 1980.

_____. "The Significance of Jacques Lacan." *Psychoanalytic Quarterly* 46 (1977): 201–19.

Loewald, Hans W. "On the Therapeutic Action of Psycho-Analysis." *International Journal of Psycho-Analysis* 41, pt. 1 (January–February 1960): 16–33.

Malcolm, Janet. "J'Appelle un Chat un Chat." *New Yorker* (20 April 1987): 84–102.

Martz, Louis. *The Poetry of Meditation.* Rev. ed. New Haven: Yale University Press, 1962.

Melville, Herman. *Moby-Dick* (1851). Edited by Luther S. Mansfield and Howard P. Vincent. New York: Hendricks House, 1952.

Miller, J. Hillis. *Fiction and Repetition: Seven English Novels.* Cambridge, Mass.: Harvard University Press, 1982.

Miller, Perry. *The New England Mind: The Seventeenth Century.* Cambridge, Mass.: Harvard University Press, 1939.

Moore, Merrill. *M: One Thousand Autobiographical Sonnets.* New York: Harcourt, Brace, 1938.

Morgan, Edmund S. *Visible Saints: The History of a Puritan Idea.* New York: New York University Press, 1963.

Nachman, Larry David. "Psychoanalysis and Social Theory: The Origin of Society and of Guilt." *Salmagundi,* nos. 52–53 (Spring–Summer 1981): 65–106.

Nims, John Frederick. *Western Wind: An Introduction to Poetry.* New York: Random House, 1974.

Olney, James. *Metaphors of Self: The Meaning of Auto-biography.* Princeton: Princeton University Press, 1972.

Onorato, Richard J. *The Character of the Poet: Wordsworth in* The Prelude. Princeton: Princeton University Press, 1971.

Pascal, Roy. *Design and Truth in Autobiography.* Cambridge, Mass.: Harvard University Press, 1960.

Pearce, Roy Harvey. *The Continuity of American Poetry.* Princeton: Princeton University Press, 1961.

Reik, Theodor. *Listening with the Third Ear: The Inner Experience of a Psychoanalyst.* New York: Farrar, Straus, 1949.

Riddell, Joseph. "Decentering the Image: The 'Project' of 'American' Poetics?" In *Textual Strategies: Perspectives in Post-Structuralist Criticism*, edited by Josué V. Harari, 322–58. Ithaca, N.Y.: Cornell University Press, 1979.

Rieff, Philip. *Freud: The Mind of the Moralist*. 3d ed. Chicago: University of Chicago Press, 1979.

Sarton, May. *Mrs. Stevens Hears the Mermaids Singing*. New York: Norton, 1965.

Schafer, Roy. *Narrative Actions in Psychoanalysis*. Worcester, Mass.: Clark University Press, 1981.

Silberman, Deanna I. " 'Confessional' Poetry and Psychoanalysis." Ph.D. Diss., Northwestern University, 1979.

Simpson, Eileen. *Poets in Their Youth*. New York: Random House, 1982.

Skura, Meredith Anne. *The Literary Use of the Psychoanalytic Process*. New Haven: Yale University Press, 1981.

Stafford, Jean. "An Influx of Poets." *New Yorker* (6 November 1978): 43–60.

Stevens, Wallace. "To an Old Philosopher in Rome." In *The Collected Poems*, 508–11. New York: Alfred A. Knopf, 1955.

Trilling, Lionel. "Freud and Literature." In *The Liberal Imagination: Essays on Literature and Society*, by Lionel Trilling, 34–57. New York: Viking, 1950.

Vendler, Helen. "An Intractable Metal." Rev. of *Collected Poems*, by Sylvia Plath. *New Yorker* (15 February 1982): 124–38.

Watkins, Owen C. *The Puritan Experience*. London: Routledge & Kegan Paul, 1972.

Waelder, Robert. *Basic Theory of Psychoanalysis*. New York: International Universities Press, 1960.

Wilden, Anthony. "Lacan and the Discourse of the Other." In *Speech and Language in Psychoanalysis*, by Jacques Lacan, 159–311. Originally published as *The Language of the Self: The Function of Language in Psychoanalysis*. Translated by Anthony Wilden. Baltimore: Johns Hopkins University Press, 1968.

———. Translator's introduction to *Speech and Language in Psychoanalysis*, by Jacques Lacan, vii–xix. Originally published as *The Language of the Self: The Function of Language in Psychoanalysis*. Translated by Anthony Wilden. Baltimore: Johns Hopkins University Press, 1968.

Winnicott, D. W. "Primitive Emotional Development" (1945). In *Collected Papers: Through Paediatrics to Psycho-Analysis*, by D. W. Winnicott, 145–56. London: Tavistock Publications, 1958.

Permissions

Index